D1363644

Feng Shui and the Tango

In Twelve Easy Lessons

Why Feng Shui Works and How to Make it Work for You

Ralph & Lahni DeAmicis

Cuore Libre Publishing

Feng Shui and the Tango in Twelve Easy Lessons
Why Feng Shui Works and How to Make it Work for You
Ralph & Lahni DeAmicis

Published by
Cuore Libre Publishing
Post Office Box 728
Bryn Athyn, PA 19009
orders@cuorelibrepublishing.com
www.cuorelibrepublishing.com
215-464-5149

Printed in Canada

Art work by Ralph DeAmicis

Library of Congress Control Number 00-136242
Publisher's Cataloging-in-Publication Data

DeAmicis, Ralph
        Feng Shui and the tango in twelve easy lessons: why feng shui works and how to make it work for you / Ralph & Lahni DeAmicis – 1st ed.
        p. cm.
        Includes bibliographical references.
        ISBN 1-931163-03-0
        1. Feng Shui. 2. DeAmicis, Lahni. II. Title

BF1779.F4D46 2000   133.3'337
                                QB100-901863

Table of Contents

Acknowledgments

A book like this isn't pounded out onto the word processor in a few months. It grows in an organic way, and Feng Shui and the Tango has been growing for years through thousands of consultations and workshops where we've learned as much from our clients and students as we ever taught them. So foremost we thank all of you who invited us into your homes and lives in the hope that we could help you. We have done our best, and learned much in the process.

Next we thank Carole Cherry and her husband Michael Hamilton of Digital Media Consultants, who together keep our computers placated, providing help of immeasurable value, with charm and amazing patience. We thank our team of Seminar Leaders who teach our programs, regale us with great stories, and offer such wonderful friendships. Donna Addesa, Phyllis Bucci, Marylouise Burke, Angel Giordano, Jacquellyne Giordano, Marlene Pocino, as well as their spouses, and those teachers standing in the wings. Our editor Jennifer DeFeo has our heartfelt thanks for her amazing attention to detail and diplomatic skills.

We thank our teachers and colleagues, for their willingness to share their wisdom freely, their dedication in bringing this information to society, and the sense of fun they bring to this art. We enjoy lecturing beside you and feel honored to call so many of you friends. We have learned from, and been helped by so many leaders in the field that to list them all wouldn't leave room for the rest of the book. If you feel you deserve to be acknowledged you probably do.

However we do need to mention several groups and individuals for their help, and their massive contributions to the fields of Feng Shui and Natural Healing. Dennis Fairchild and Angel Thompson, simply for being good friends and a lot of fun. James Allyn Moser and his team at Feng Shui Warehouse, especially Bill Arblaster. Marta Lucia Olano and her team in Bogata, especially Claudia Correal. Stephen Skinner, and his team at Feng Shui for Modern Living, especially Velo Mitrovich. Rob Clancey and Joy Miller and their team at the Learning Studios. Don Smyth and Dennis Roberts of RGarden, R.D.Chin, Terah Kathyrn Collins and her publisher Louise Hay, Jonathan Hulsh, Lillian Garnier, Sean Xenja, Panther Wilde, A.T.Mann, Martin Davis, Lin Yun, Elliot Tanzer, Robert & Charmion McKusick, Juan Alvarez, Helen and James Jay, Edgar Sung, Nancy Santopietro, Monica and Bruno Koppel, David Kennedy, and most especially Ken & Joan Negus, Rob Hand, John Marchesella and Michael Lutin.

We also have to thank Richard and Carol Dicks, and Larrissa Jones, great teachers, great people, great friends. And as always we thank our families, especially our children and grandchildren, for the joy and delight you share with us.

Of course we thank Mother Earth for her generosity, Father Sky for his wisdom, and the divine spirit who creates this sea of luminous life we swim in.

A Note from Ralph and Lahni and the folks at Cuore Libre Publishing

Feng Shui is a powerful tool and spiritual technology. As such it should not be treated lightly. In this book we offer you information that we have found useful, valid, and harmless. This is a deep field with an ancient history rooted in the mystery traditions of many cultures. The issues we discuss here and the techniques we describe are based upon sound principles, good sense, and extensive personal experience.

However this is not a consultation. A book can not analyze your specific issues, nor provide solutions tailored to your needs and personality. This book is meant to educate and hopefully entertain. The authors and Cuore Libre Publishing shall have neither liability nor responsibility to any person or entity with respect to any loss or damage caused, or alleged to have been caused, directly or indirectly, by the information contained in this book. If you do not wish to be bound by the above, you may return this book to the publisher for a full refund.

That said, if you find that you're dealing with issues that we discuss here, and really feel you need help, consult a competent professional in the field. On the other hand, a great deal of what we might call Feng Shui common sense is easy to learn and do for yourself. But be careful. Make changes gradually. If you change too many things at once and your life goes off the edge, how are you going to know which change caused it, so you can push it back again? And finally, if everything in your life is going great, don't move anything, change will happen soon enough. It's the nature of the Universe.

Feng Shui and the Tango in Twelve Easy Lessons

Introduction
What's in it For Me?
Or Why You Might Need this Book

Now before you start flipping through the pages looking for the dance diagrams, let's explain the title. Feng Shui and the Tango developed over five years through hundreds of workshops, and thousands of consultations. During our early seminars many people came to us complaining that they had read some books on Feng Shui, and now were completely confused. Many of the early books in the field were very arcane, which is another word for secretive, and coming from the mystery schools, they didn't explain why Feng Shui worked. Also the books made little or no adjustment for a western audience, so unless you had a pretty good background in a variety of esoteric fields, you could find yourself out of your depth pretty quickly. At the time we started teaching Feng Shui we had a lot of experience with the difficulties of guiding people through three-dimensional arts, through our work in sculpture, ceramics and assorted other crafts and skills. The early books faced quite a challenge, and considering everything they did pretty well. But for most people they didn't make the concepts come alive.

When we were asked about this information gap we got into the habit of saying that learning Feng Shui through most books was like trying to learn the Tango through a correspondence course. Feng Shui and the Tango are both multi-dimensional arts. Dance diagrams are fine, but you don't do the Tango with just your feet. Feng Shui is about more than just moving furniture and hanging chimes. It's about how your body and soul fill your daily, evolving world. No matter how much reading you do, to know either one intimately, eventually you have to get out there on the dance floor and do it. In Feng Shui you have to make the changes in your home or work place, and see, and feel the changes they make in your life. So from the earliest articles and seminar manuals this evolved from, our book was always known as *Feng Shui and the Tango, in Twelve Easy Lessons.*

Fortunately in recent years some very useful, and accessible books have come upon the scene. Yet, even those of you who are quite well read in the field will find that there're some things in Tango that are unique, and very helpful for doing Feng Shui at a more advanced, and more effective level. We guess we could have called this book Power Feng Shui, but it would still be *Feng Shui and the Tango* in our hearts.

We've sought to make our book as experiential as possible, much like our workshops. We've used a lot of material that we've presented to groups of people that produced that look in their eyes that said "Ah ha, now I understand!" We've also included some deeper concepts showing the connection between the Asian and Western systems, so you can put this knowledge into a familiar context. We approach teaching Feng Shui in a style designed to help you to easily retain the methods, and then apply them in practical situations in your own life. We do this by explaining the underlying principles at work in modern terms, then demonstrating it with the occasional story, and filling in with lots of drawings and diagrams. Our aim is that you'll understand the players and the game so well, that when issues arise outside of the situations we describe, you'll know how to address them.

Keep in mind that we tag-team lecture, so we jump back and forth from topic to topic. We seem to repeat ourselves, because we do, when it's a very important concept. But when we do, we're actually approaching the same subject again from a different angle. Each time we'll fill in another facet, color in another function and round out your understanding of the essentials. We want to help you get comfortable with the idea that you have the power to create positive change in your life very quickly.

The techniques that we bring up again and again, are those that will easily create that change. Yet they're the same ones that people often resist doing. Why? It's not that they're complicated or difficult to do. Truthfully they're very easy to accomplish. A lot of Feng Shui is very easy to do. What's often hard for people is feeling comfortable with change. That discomfort comes from not feeling familiar with the steps that create the change that they desire. Or feeling that they don't deserve better than they have. We're going to share the steps with you, and explain why they work. Then if you'll make the changes, you'll find that your feelings improve for the better. The next thing you know improvements will be happening in your life at a wonderful pace, because you took action, the correct action.

We've had people come up to us many times and tell us that our seminar dramatically improved their life. We'd say

"That's great. Who are you?" because we wouldn't recognize them. They'd say "Oh, I didn't take your class myself, but my friend did, and they told me all about it, and I made some changes and my life is so much better, thank you." How hard could Feng Shui be if it works so well second hand?

Some of Tango is quite basic, and some is a bit advanced. But don't worry, even when we get into the fancy dance steps we'll hold your hand. We've put a lot of effort into making the concepts easy to understand and easy to apply. This approach was developed through hundreds of workshops with thousands of people. Some of the material is right out of our early seminars. Other parts evolved through a lot of late night discussions, and trying it out with the next group of students.

Chapters 1,2 & 3 build up the basic concepts. Chapter 4, the Bagua, shows you the map of life in surprisingly practical detail. Chapter 5 recognizes that you're getting anxious to move the furniture around, and get out there on the dance floor, so we offer you some Immediate Solutions. In Chapter 6, the Feng Shui Tool Box, while you catch your breath from moving the heavy stuff, we're going to lay out the tools and show you how to use them. In Chapter 7, the Universal Checklist, we're going to discuss people's favorite problems, and how to resolve them. In Chapter 8 we'll give you a modern primer on colors. In Chapter 9, the Powers of the Earth, we start adding some fancy moves, and in Chapter 10, the Stars of Home, hold onto your hats because we take some real leaps. But don't worry, in Chapter 11, the Geometry of Survival, we get back to the fun stuff, and in Chapter 12, Herstory, we'll catch our breath, and you'll hear our own mildly irreverent slant on how this art evolved globally.

As you use this knowledge please remember that in any

healing art, there are two important qualities that you need to encourage, compassion and a sense of humor. Compassion is important for the sake of the people you give advice to. That includes yourself. A sense of humor is important, because in the practice of this art we may see situations that are wonderful, incredible, tragic, and bizarre. Compassion for others impels you to pursue this art, but only an excellent sense of humor allows you to. It gives you the lightness of spirit necessary, to keep delving into the mysteries that so perplex people's lives.

In creating this book we've taken off our well worn consulting hats and the necessary inhibitions they require, and put on our comfy lecturers' gowns. As a result our senses of humor are happily more able to prance about and insinuate themselves into the material. It's been our experience that the best practitioners, and we've know many of them, are very funny people. That's not surprising since Feng Shui is a very funny field. Many times late at night over dinner, after a lecture, we've come up with all kinds of odd philosophical questions.

For example, a dozen years ago most people hadn't heard of Feng Shui. Yet today it's simultaneously the name of a discipline; "The Art of Feng Shui," a title; "The Feng Shui Man," a verb; "We were Feng Shui-ing all day, and boy are we beat!" an adjective; "That place was a Feng Shui nightmare!", and a compliment; "You've got great Feng Shui". These days Feng Shui seems to be weaving itself into all kinds of places. So when some lovely soul smiles at you invitingly and asks "Why don't you come on up and Feng Shui me sometime?" Aren't you going to be glad that you have this book? With Feng Shui all is possible, and potentially delightful.

It's a good thing that Feng Shui has a funny side, because it helps balance out the profound wisdom and

5

mysticism that the art is blessed with. Feng Shui doesn't lack for depth, grace or beauty. Great age has only increased its luster. Its hallmark is its ability to create balance within the motion of life.

If you feel that Feng Shui is a very serious subject, and our humor, or modern approach, at any time offends you, we beg your forgiveness. On the other hand we're quite unwilling to abandon our humor or change our approach. It's not that we don't take our subject seriously. We do within reason! Our humor serves to illuminate a subject we love teaching, and it's a reflection of the joy we find in the practice of this art.

What is Feng Shui? Transliterated from the Mandarin and phonetically pronounced "fung shway", it literally means wind and water. In nature it's these two elements that change the world. Water dissolves the mountains into sand, and the wind reshapes that into dunes. Feng Shui is the art of placing yourself in the most advantageous place to benefit from the many dimensions of the Earth's evolving process. This powerful art is known by many other names throughout the world, and if a culture doesn't practice it, that culture doesn't prosper, nor possibly survive. No matter the name, it's a system for creating vital balance in our environments.

At its best, Feng Shui is a mix of ancient techniques and modern knowledge. It works with the body's original programming as a blueprint to shape our living spaces into dynamic tools that serve our future rather than hold us in the past. It's as practical as it is mystical, and as modern as it is primal. It mirrors the role our bodies play as vehicles for our spirit.

The purpose of Feng Shui is to create harmony, balance, and healthy growth. But like a thunderstorm that clears the air, permitting all things to be renewed, Feng Shui recognizes that directed change is necessary to allow the beauty of life, so easily obscured, to shine through.

Sometimes simply repositioning a chair, moving a bed, or putting a picture on a desk is enough to make a person's energy smile in that space. Other times, a major shift, along with some sweat and sore muscles, is necessary to break up old patterns and to guide the Chi, the breath of life, into new pathways.

But still the question remains: "Sure the system's been working great for 5,000 years, what's it done for me lately?" In the words of the ancient Chinese fortuneteller, good Feng Shui can bring you love, money, and good luck. In our words, it helps get the old junk and destructive tensions out of your life. Next, it invites in those energies that will give you satisfaction, a sense of joy, and validation for your efforts. This is important because your environments tend to reinforce who you were, not necessarily who you want to be.

So what are the techniques we use to change those emotional dungeons into spiritual havens? Well, that's what this book is about, but here's a hint: If you're reading this book sitting with your back to the door, you need to read Chapter 1. If you're in a relationship with communication problems, you need to read Chapter 7. If you have a bedroom you can't sleep in, or a family room you can't get everybody in the family together in, or an office you hate to work in, you really need to read Chapter 11, a few times. We're going to help you learn how to listen to your body more effectively, how to understand what your surroundings are telling you, and how to create harmony within movement, in your home and work place.

The methods we use are drawn from the major schools of Feng Shui, as well as Geomancy, the Western art used for thousands of years to place and design buildings. Sacred Geometry is the foundation of the Geomantic arts, and it describes the relationships between the human and the divine, the Earth and the Sky, the seen and the unseen. We also talk about modern ergonomics, which is the art of designing environments to fit the human form. We touch upon horizon-based Astrology, the three-dimensional system that shares the same foundations as the Asian Compass School of Feng Shui.

We also explain the workings of the Bagua, which is the map of environmental space. The Bagua is traditionally divided into eight parts, and it serves as Feng Shui's primary philosophical and practical tool. Our approach to the Bagua may seem revolutionary, but in truth it draws upon ancient sources, and is adapted for modern times and Western styles. Here's a hint: We divide the space into twelve parts instead of eight, and we go into much greater detail concerning the areas of money, love, and marriage. The chapter on the Bagua is a must for anyone concerned with love and money, or money and love, or both. In other words: everybody.

Before you throw up your hands screaming that this is too much to attempt to learn, relax, and understand that because of our approach you'll find identifying problem areas simple, and applying the solutions surprisingly easy. We clearly explain in modern, practical terms why something is causing you trouble and how to heal it. When you feel the improvement in your emotions, in your body and in the people around you, it's like dancing. When the energies are flowing smoothly it feels like magic. And once you learn Feng Shui and the Tango, you'll never want to forget it.

Chapter One
The
Intimate Lair
What Your Home is Doing for You

Imagine you're in one of our seminars. We're standing in front of you. Ralph, the taller one, holds up a pair of timbale, which are magical Tibetan bells. He strikes them together, and the song spreads out and paints the room, leaving behind a blissful silence. In that special space he says, "We start every workshop with the sound of chimes." And here he taps them together, and they sing again.

In the shadow of their song he continues, "Their song reminds us that while these chimes are solid, they translate into a vibrational world." He taps the chimes together again and mimics the sound waves spreading out with an undulating wave of his hand towards you, "In the same way that our bodies are solid." Here he slaps his thigh a couple of times, "they translate into a vibrational world." Then Lahni, who is smaller but prettier, says: "As each of us came through that doorway, we painted the doorway, the frame, and the pathway with our energy." She smiles and says: "So all you could hope for when you entered this room is that the person who came in before you was in a good mood, because you're going to pick up some of their energy. We're going to teach you to more effectively manage and color that energy that gets painted on your environment so it better serves your purposes."

This is the real Feng Shui, this is the real Geomancy, this is the real Earth Magic. This is the secret language that your body speaks to your environment in, and with which your home, office, bedroom, and garden answers you. As Feng Shui consultants we are not healers. We are translators. The language is there in your genetic codes. The words are programmed into your blood. It is a three-dimensional dialect that you understood perfectly as a little child. Your command of it may have been lost along with your childlike sense of discovery. If it has gone astray, wake up! Turn on those forgotten codes in your blood. Stretch those corners of your eyes that once saw nature spirits and faces in the trees and waterfalls. How did you get into this sorry condition? We ask this like Peter Pan confronting a grown-up Wendy, "How did you lose your ability to fly?"

Somewhere along our path to a modern world, people lost track of a few essential magical truths. First, we are human, we are animal, but we are also magical, and full of both brilliance and basic needs. We thrive on daily allotments of certain things such as light, color, fresh air, and clean water. We need environments where we can relax, and daily be able to get away from that constant tension that we, as members of a modern society, wear as a badge of honor. Every day we need to feed our emotions as well as our bodies.

Empower the feelings of your body, ignore the thoughts in your head. Remember walking into places that just "felt right?" Remember other times where your nose told you to "turn around and leave" and you did! You were practicing Feng Shui right there, and you didn't even know it. Have you ever almost endlessly rearranged your furniture, only stopping when it felt good? Why didn't the first dozen arrangements satisfy you? They didn't feel good. This one felt better! That's exactly the point. We do the most important things by feeling, just like every other creature in this garden. Here's a hint: Our bodies are much more in touch with our feelings than our minds. Trust your body: it rarely lies.

Consider the denizens of your intimate lair. If your cat is napping on your bed, probably on your expensive silk pajamas, you can pretty much bet that kitty's head is facing the doorway. Why? Because she can't relax unless she knows that the second she hears a footfall, she has only to slit one lazy eye to check out the intruder. If it's someone suspicious, maybe of the canine persuasion, she's ready to dart out of there! If it's her pet human, that's another matter entirely. But it's only when Miss Kitty can comfortably command the entrance way that she can feel secure enough to close those baby blues and catch 40 winks.

Which brings us to the first principle, "Command the door." Do you think that we are really any different from that cuddly feline? You never really feel comfortable with your back to the door.

Whenever we walk into a room, we lay down that pathway of energy, painting it with the colors from our personal field. Remember: We have to live with those colors we create. After a time the people walking through a house carve an energetic stream that affects everyone and everything there. One reason your body resists relaxing with your back turned is that the doorway is the fountain nozzle of that energy stream. The spine is your body's primary electrical pathway. It reads this disruptive energy of the entrance and feels vulnerable to any saber-toothed tigers that may be lurking outside. It doesn't matter to your body that you consciously know that the alarm is on, the dogs are watching, and for all intents and purposes, you are safe. Your animal body doesn't care about the silly musings of your conscious mind. It knows what it feels.

If your body can't command the entrance to your "intimate lair" and feel able to respond quickly to any threat that appears there, you stay tense on a subtle but profound level. Remember: your mind will lie to you about survival issues. But your body won't. Believing your head and ignoring your body can be a major cause of chaos in your life! After all, Feng Shui is a magical

Your Aura is your paint brush. The inner field relates to the physical body, The middle is the emotional body and the outer is the mental/ spiritual energies

dance. When you go spinning across the floor, it's all body and soul. Dancing is akin to falling in love: It's wraps you up in beauty and carries you along. When the Feng Shui is great, you glow. Logic and reason aren't even on the floor.

In the Asian tradition it's said that the three most important places in a house are the front door, the stove, and the bed. The front door is your face upon the world. The stove is your place of nurturing. The bed is important because it's where you restore yourself. To those three we would add the desk, probably because we spend so much time sitting at ours. The desk relates to how you communicate, how you do business, and how you think about the world. What we've been talking about in this chapter is the relationship between the door and these very important parts of your life. If the door to your house or to your room represents your responsibilities to the outside world, the way in which you physically relate to that door will pattern how you relate to those responsibilities.

Where are the most important places this dynamic will affect you? The kitchen! What kind of tension is being served with your favorite meals when the stove position doesn't allow the cook to command the door? Many families don't cook because of a badly placed stove. This fragments the close, personal relationship. Food tastes better when it's infused with comfort and love. Your desk! How can you concentrate on doing your best work if you're tense because you're sitting with your back to a door or walkway? The bedroom! How can you get a good night's sleep if your body is on alert because your bed position doesn't let you command the door? (Note: Later we discuss placing the bed in relation to the compass directions. This is important, so read the section on directions before you start moving the heavy furniture.) You can dramatically improve your attitude about the outside world and your ability to handle stress if

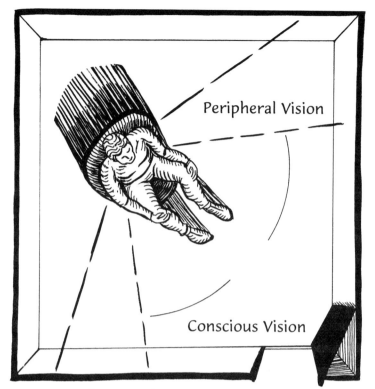

Commanding the Door Means
Using the Central Part of the Visual Range

you make a point of taking a commanding position whenever you can.

What if you can't move your desk, or your bed is nailed to the floor? That's what mirrors are for. Your body is smart and knows how to use a rear-view mirror. Who says they're only for cars? They work great on desks, stoves, and in all types of places. In the tool chapter, we discuss mirrors in great detail, but for now consider that what you see is what your body believes, and what you see is up to you to decide.

Chapter Two
Catching Your Attention
How to Create Your Program for Success

To your body, every doorway is an invitation to enter a brand new place, no matter how many times you've been there before. This is because for the body there is no future, there is no past, there is only this crystalline moment, this now. Some entrance ways are more inviting to your body than others. Why is that? It depends upon how focused the entrance experience is.

Have you ever gone to meet someone in an unfamiliar restaurant, or better yet, a strange bar? How do you feel when you go inside? Your eyes dart around the room searching for someone or something familiar. Anything will do, even that big neon eagle above the bar. At least it's something you can focus on until your eye finds something more appealing, like your friends sitting over there in that corner booth. You see their smiling faces, and your body takes you where your eyes are pointed. You're like a runner headed for home. Then you're plopping down in your chair amid a swirl of keys and coats. Safe! It makes your body tense if you walk through a doorway and there's nothing definite for you to focus on immediately.

As long as your eyes are in motion without a focus, the fight-or-flight reflex stays turned on. Try this for yourself. Move your eyes back and forth without letting them settle on anything for even a moment. Watch where tension shifts to in your body. It will rise up in your chest and hover there. This is your body's preparation for fight-or-flight. When your eyes find that friendly face, your energy settles back down into your belly. You relax.

What does this little experiment tell us? That every room needs a strong-colored focal point for your eyes to go to in order to turn off that disruptive fight-or-flight energy as soon as possible. Otherwise the entrance way becomes soaked in this static charge losing its focus, and with that, a sense of purpose. When choosing the subject for the focus, realize that the body believes what it sees. The image you choose will create the program your body accepts. (Choose carefully! If you use a strong color, remember that color has a profound influence on you, based upon its own language that we explain in detail in Chapter Eight.)

Here's an action step using color. If you have a space that is absolutely chaotic and feel the need for an immediate improvement, consider that red is the most effective single color for catching the eye. Another way to gain attention is to use the most powerful contrasting colors: yellow and black.

Red boosts the heart beat, sets off the autonomic nervous system, makes the vision sharper, the sense of smell more sensitive, and hearing more acute. Yellow does this to a lesser extent. Yellow also produces clarity of thought. The extremes of the eye's visual range are the yellow of day and the black of night, so the eye finds this contrast easy to distinguish. Using either red or yellow and black as a focus will pull all of the attention towards them and force the space into a more concentrated program. One caveat here: If you really don't like red or yellow and black, don't use them as a focus. Just make sure that the focus contains strong enough color and contrast to completely catch your attention.

Make sure that the subject matter of your focus is inspiring and uplifting. A picture of people who love you looking happy works pretty well. If the focus is in a business environment, the first contact image needs to support the goals of the endeavor. This is where company logos and pictures of products come in handy. You actively program the room by your choice of subject, so be aware of the programming you're choosing. Be aware that when someone has a history of living with difficult, critical people, they may be inclined to keep employing those kinds of images. They should feel free to change them as fast as they can. One of the great things about Feng Shui techniques is their ability to improve things immediately. Never underestimate the power an image has to program you, nor the value of making the changes now.

So let's review the essentials. If a room doesn't have a definite focus for the eye when you first enter, the room loses focus and chaos takes over. Why? Because the most powerful energy in a room is your human, electrical energy! When you walk into a room, you paint it with the living vitality contained in your aura and your vision. If the room lacks a visual focus, everyone who enters goes into the fight-or-flight mode. They spray their stressful energy all over the place like a watering hose with a broken nozzle. The cumulative vibrations painted around the doorway become increasingly discordant and disruptive. After a while anyone entering the room, even with their eyes closed, will feel that unpleasant tension. To your body fight-or-flight means "Drop everything and run". If you don't have a clear focus this explains why everything you carry in gets dumped on the table by the door just before you dash for the safety of the kitchen. That refrigerator is a great focal point, isn't it? To say nothing of the leftover lasagna!

How do you create order in your environment? By creating a natural hierarchy. Nature is created with a practical structure that allows for everything to have its own place. That focal point becomes the central theme that everything else fits around. If you don't create that energized structure in your space, you invite in chaos. Chaos is normally something you want to avoid, except maybe in the guestroom. One thing we always want you to remember: Don't make your guestroom too comfortable. Ignore this advice and one day a few weeks into their visit you'll overhear your 'weekend guests' complaining about the shabby rugs and drapes in their room.

In the section on the Bagua, we're going to show you how to create order in your environment by using the natural map of interior spaces. Where the visual focus is placed upon this map can have a profound influence by powerfully activating a specific theme or component of your life. That's why we're emphasizing the importance of catching and guiding your attention. That's why the images you encounter when you go through that door are some of the most powerful tools you can use in this magical dance.

Of course there're two sides to every coin. While monochromatic environments can produce spaces so crammed with clutter that the whole place becomes a disordered blur, homes with too many beautiful things diverting your eye can lead you on an endless merry-go-round of diversions. A room stuffed to capacity with beautiful art can be like a stage full of great Divas. No one wants to step aside and let another shine. Amid the beautiful blaze you may lose sight of the symbols that guide you and tie your life together. That unified, but structured theme is what creates an environment that helps you manifest your long-term goals.

Do you want some suggestions for a good focus? Simple! Any image that makes you happy and contains sufficiently strong color or contrast that your eyes are irresistibly drawn to when you first enter the room. If it's in the kitchen, let it be images of food or sharing. For the living room, select a picture that depicts socializing and comfort. In the bedroom, the images need to be relaxing. In the couple's bedroom, the focus could include some sensuality and romantic pairing, assuming that's what you'd like happening in there now and then. By the way, no family photos in the bedroom. You don't want to feel like your parents, children, grandparents and assorted aunts, uncles and cousins, are watching what's going on in there.

For an office, a focus on the company name and logo tells you where you are and what you're there for. It increases productivity, efficiency, and should inspire you. The word inspiration (like aesthetic) comes from the Greek word for breath. The Chinese word Chi means among other things, the breath of life. Experiencing beauty may provoke a sudden intake of breath. This is the soul's reaction to encountering the sublime in a lover's face, beautiful art, and nature in her subtle magnificence.

The more we study the body, the more we realize it's magical. To your body, the image is almost as powerful as the object itself. Even though your inspiration may only be a complex, colored pattern on a slip of paper or a canvas, as in a painting or a photo, what your body sees is a smiling face, or a rainbow over cascading falls. So place that instrument of inspiration where you'll encounter it daily, and let its power to uplift you be released. Soon that entrance-way will glow with the accumulated good feelings that have been painted on it by the aura of everyone walking in and experiencing it.

What type of focus do you want to avoid? Leaving your unpaid bills on a side table just inside your front door, or seeing the garbage can or the laundry basket as the first things to greet you. These are sure ways to sabotage the joy of your homecoming. Walk into each room and see where your eyes go first. Stop blundering about, unaware of the images and objects that are triggering your emotions. They program your subconscious in constant and subtle ways.

Keep this in mind about images and symbols. The Universe is very literal, and it definitely has a sense of humor! When you invite the universal energy into your space, you are absolutely telling the Universe what you desire in every area of your life. If the Universe sees images that are chaotic, it says, "Hmmm, they want some chaos, I can give them that!" If you forget about a strong focus, the next thing you know, your office looks like the inside of a trash compactor. The images in your pictures, figurines, photos, the pattern in the fabrics, all add items on to your wish list. You then hand over your requests to the Universe to provide them for you. It does, and the next thing you're saying is, "Oops. Did I ask for that?" Yes, you probably did!

Is that all there is to it? Not really, there's more! Visual clues are not the only messages you respond to. Do you remember the first time you smelled fresh-baked bread? How did that make you feel? Pretty good! Remember that "inspiration" means taking a breath. The correct scent will raise your energy levels. On the other hand, do you recall walking into a place to eat when it didn't "smell right"? The next thing you knew, you were back in your car looking for some place else to eat. The sense of smell is physical and primal. For this sense to function, a particle of the object has to travel through the air and land in your nose. Then it has to be interpreted by the emotional part of the brain. That's why scents can be so sensual and intimate.

A baby recognizes its mother by her scent. The familiar fragrances of home are as important to your emotional wellbeing as loving arms and a comfy chair. Needless to say, dirty laundry or garbage near the door is a Feng Shui faux pas. On the other hand, the power of home cooking to enrich the emotions reaches you through your nose as you walk through the front door, long before it reaches your lips at the kitchen table.

Just because you've gone through that door a hundred times and your mind is oblivious to the discordant images and scents, your body is not. It reacts with tension and anxiety at every encounter, because it's programmed to be ever vigilant to threats, sharp angles, discord, and strange smells! This is the stuff of survival, and the body takes it very seriously. The continual play of tensions the body experiences as it adapts to the environment influences the conscious mind in subtle and not-so-subtle ways. As we continue, you'll find many examples of the physiological and psychological results of environmental disharmony and the benefits you can experience by shaping your spaces with conscious sensitivity.

Here are some stories about imagery and placement. We had a client with a lovely oil painting in the health section of her bedroom. Don't worry, in chapter 4 we're going to tell you which sections relate to health. It was a still life with a bowl of fruit, and she was puzzled as to why her health seemed to be so fragile. "Fruit is healthy. Isn't it a great image for this section?" she asked. We in turn asked, "What happens to fruit in about a week?" She was dumbfounded. We explained that it's either eaten or it spoils. In either case, fruit has only a very short period of perfection. Remember how literal the Universe is. That image says, "Here today, gone tomorrow!" That is not what she wanted for her state of health, but it was what she was asking for. What's a better image for the health section? A photo of an evergreen forest! It's sturdy, always green, growing, vital, and strong. The perfect image for health is one of vitality and longevity rather than of something temporary and fleeting.

Of course, we know this from personal experience. After months of struggling with the most perplexing health issues, we were at our wits ends. Every time we would make some progress, something else would pop out of left field, and the puzzle would take on a new twist. We've been herbalists for many years, after all. We should be able to plot a smoother path. Finally, while standing in the doorway to our bedroom, Ralph casually observed: "I'm not sure that Escher print (one of his incredible stairway mazes with the changing perspectives...are you going up the stairs or down the stairs?) placed in the health section of our bedroom is quite the image we want there, are you?" This image literally described the obstacle course we were traveling in search of vibrant health. Feng Shui Man, heal thyself! Now the question became: "Where do you place such an unusual picture?" With a little imagination, we found the perfect spot for it. On a central staircase from which you could choose to go either up or down.

Sometimes, the image is inappropriate altogether. When teenagers cover the walls with depressing and self-defeating imagery, it's no surprise that they lose the motivation to find joy in their lives and aspire toward a bright future. Sometimes it's the job of the parent to edit the images thoughtfully. If the kids object, parents should negotiate. If the kids ask for a reason, tell them that it comes direct from the Feng Shui Wizards! One of the secrets in life is knowing what to trust, and its amazing how many children, including teenagers trust Feng Shui. They're a lot smarter than many people think.

Chapter Three
The Art of Chi
The Nature of the Life Force

In the many, many, many, lectures that we've attended, we've heard the top Feng Shui practitioners talk about Chi. What is Chi anyway, and why is it so important? Can you buy it at the store, online, or through a catalog, 1-800-CHI-SHOP? Or is it one of those things that you have to make yourself, like a really good apple pie? Whatever the answer, the real question is, "What has it done for you lately?" The next question is, "Once you get some Chi, will you know what to do with it?" Don't worry, all your questions will be answered. We're also going to teach you how to attract it and how to guide it. We're going to explain how it behaves and what it can do for you when it gets here?

Well, the long and the short of it is, as we mentioned before, Chi is the breath of life. It's also known as Qi, Prana, Ether, or Life Force. It is an essential energy that every cohesive being on the planet possesses, whether that's a person, an animal, a tree, a wind, a cloud, or a rock. What makes Chi? That takes some explaining. We live on a round planet, Earth, and she has a tremendous amount of energy expressed in her spinning orbit around the Sun, and in the force we notice the most, gravity. We're part of a solar system filled with diverse elements. You might say that every body in the Universe puts their own spin on it, they each have a unique energy that affects every other body according to its size and relative distance. On Earth, that energy flows in a circular pattern, since she is a round planet that both rotates and orbits our Sun. The Moon and the planets repeat these circular motions, creating the songs we call the cycles of life. This symphony of motion, this music of the spheres, creates the energetic flow that we call Chi, the divine breath that sings the song of life. With our breath, we contribute to that symphony.

How does it behave? When Chi enters a room it flows in a circular pattern, moving in a clockwise direction. This means that as it enters a typical room, it veers to the left initially and works its way around to the right. In the process it sets up a series of polarities. We might describe this sequence of poles as the notes that create the music of that space. In shaping that room with walls and objects, a unique song is created that you then live with and dance to, whether you realize that or not. Generally it's a good idea to be conscious of the tune you're creating day to day, with your art, your furniture, and your clutter.

It might help to know that each note relates to a specific area of your aura and a specific part of your life. The map of this special relationship is shown in the Bagua. (*Ba* means eight, *Qua* means trigram) The trigrams are found in the Chinese *Book of Changes*, the I Ching. The trigrams are symbolic of the various roles we each play in the game through the cycles of time.

Ergonomic designers create the floor plans for supermarkets are aware of this directional flow through a reverse logic. Studies have shown that if customers enter at the right side of a store and work their way

24

counterclockwise, they spend more money. Why? They are walking continually against the natural clockwise flow of energy into the space and it slows them down, so they spend more time in the aisles. This is especially useful if you want to sell people things that they don't necessarily need.

Think about your favorite stores, places that are easy to shop. They'll follow the opposite philosophy, and you'll probably find that their traffic flow directs you around to the left, moving clockwise from the entrance. Professional organizers tell their clients to straighten up their spaces in a clockwise direction, because their studies have shown that to be more efficient.

It's helpful to understand the inherent structure of energy. All vibration, whether it's light, sound, heat, gravity, or electromagnetic signatures from humans, animals, plants and minerals, adheres to a basic system. As an example, when light goes through a refracting crystal, it breaks up into a series of colors or tones, creating a rainbow. Is the sequential pattern of colors ever different? No. The order of the colors is consistent every time. When energy flows into a room through a doorway and curves around the space, it establishes a series of tones, like musical notes. That series of musical notes is the *Bagua*. It works in a primal pattern that is the same every time, because it's the basic pattern of energy that underlies and creates order for life on Earth and in our particular part of the Universe.

This familiarity and consistency of structure is what

modern ergonomic, industrial, and interior designers aim for. This is true whether they're creating a hotel room, a telephone, or a car. Alas! Gone are the days of that helpful bell boy who would show you around your suite, explaining all of its wonders and secrets, gratefully accepting any gifts you would care to bestow upon him. Now everything needs to be in a familiar and recognizable place. Your overnight stop needs to be just like every other hotel room you've ever been in, with no additional instructions necessary and no surprises. Good designers simply strive to make us feel comfortable. Any good design needs to include the universal principles of balanced movement through complementary polarities. This is what we call Yin and Yang.

So do you want to understand how the Bagua works and how it can work for you? That means getting into the details, which requires breaking out of the current paradigm. Because the Bagua that's been used for hundreds of years is a bit indistinct, a little fuzzy, and while it's perfect for an ancient Chinese Sage, the concept is way out of its depths when it comes to working efficiently in a modern Western Society. If you're familiar with the traditional pattern of the Bagua, hold on to your hat, because we're upping the stakes. If this concept of the Bagua is all new to you, that's great. That way there's nothing for you to unlearn.

Let's start off with the big picture by explaining that the Asian Bagua is essentially the Chinese Astrological house system brought down to Earth. Astrological house systems are maps of the heavens in relation to Earth, and this includes the Asian, Indian and Western systems. As maps they include compass directions. At the same time they are maps of the human energy field, the physical aura. It is a map of that pattern of tones that we paint in our environments. Does this sound mysterious? Guess what?

These maps or charts were developed by what are called the Mystery schools. When passing on the knowledge it was not uncommon for parts to be left out, making it even more mysterious. How did they develop their systems? They observed the natural world and created these systems to understand the workings of this five-dimensional process that we call time. These house systems became the foundational, philosophical tools of cultures throughout the world. We're going to put the Bagua aside for the moment. In chapter four we'll explain it in much greater detail, but for now let's work on getting you over some bumps on the road to harmonious homes.

Now Chi is no simple thing. First it's made up of its two major components, Yin and Yang, remember them?

Understanding the ins and outs of Yin and Yang is a never-ending process for the Feng Shui aficionado. This ancient concept of the polarities is so beautiful and poetic that we always include it as a part of our lectures, but it's important to bring the workings of Yin and Yang down to Earth into everyday life. Clarifying this concept is not always easy, but it is necessary because the power of your solutions depends upon your ability to understand the interplay of Yin and Yang. This understanding allows us to apply the concept in diverse situations. In our modern society, we question everything, not content to follow the obedient compliance of a by-gone era. If we understand what we're trying to accomplish when we start moving the furniture, we'll be able to more easily get some help with the heavy stuff, and the solutions will be far more effective.

The major stumbling block in explaining Yin and Yang

has to do with helping people unlearn some old thinking. Yin and Yang don't simply equate to feminine and masculine, bad and good, and so on. They really don't equate to positive and negative, which are engineering and scientific terms. Yin and Yang exist in a different context and are ultimately more complex. The most accurate English correlation is the polarity of responsive and dynamic. All of us and all things in our environment display both of these qualities at one time or another, in various amounts. Can things be almost equally Yin and Yang? Of course they can! But usually not for long, change happens.

Warning! Dangerous Philosophical Curves Ahead! If you don't want the detailed, excruciatingly technical explanation for this conceptual amplification, also known as Ralph's "Mr. Segue Spot", you might want to skip the next paragraph.

The misunderstanding of Yin and Yang as negative and positive is akin to modern science's mistranslation of the ancient elements that Aristotle described. Fire, air, earth, and water do not relate to the atomic measurements of hydrogen, copper, and iron, and so on, or what science calls the elements on the periodic table today. It's naive to think that ancient societies capable of creating such marvels as Stonehenge, the Coliseum, and the Pyramids, did not understand the essential nature of metal, earth, and gases. The ideas that were translated as the ancient elements are better understood as the four states of matter: plasma, gaseous, solid, and liquid. Ancient systems of knowledge were concerned with understanding how the natural world conducted the process of one element transforming into another in the continuous flow of Chi: energy, cosmic breath, the story of life. Hey, you wanted to know!

Yang is the motivating force, the dynamic movement, and the external influence. It is essentially masculine. Yin is the responding receptivity, reactive adjustment, and internal

modulation. It is essentially feminine. In
our work it is essential to remember
that just as the masculine will
always move towards the feminine,
Yang will always move towards
Yin. Yin will in turn accept and
intermingle with Yang, seeking a
harmonious mean, a neutral balance.

Imagine having a bright, sunny
kitchen charged with the energy of a busy family, and it has
a door leading into a dark and damp basement. Whenever
the door is open, a subtle energetic flow will develop from
the Yang brightness of the kitchen down into the dark Yin of
the basement. Why else do you think Mom will keep closing
that door while muttering under her breath, "Why can't
anyone ever shut this door?" She feels the drain on her
energy.

Do you have a bathroom attached to your bedroom and
(tsk! tsk!) do you leave the door open at night? The flow
continually draws your Yang energy while you're asleep in
the bedroom towards the receptive water in the toilet
and the traps of the sink and bath. When you
flush after that midnight sojourn, there goes
your energy down the drain. Oops! Kind of
explains why you wake up more tired
than when you went to sleep.

A less obvious example: A
shallow stream or underground
spring cutting across the
resource section of your lot or
house (the far left-hand
corner) will tap away the
stabilizing energy, often
leading to a never-

ending list of expensive repairs. The phrase "Money Pit" comes to mind! The frustrating thing about this configuration is that you will feel obligated to dump even more money into the property to get it ready for sale, and you'll invariably spend a lot on things that won't earn your money back. Then you complain about money always flowing through your fingers. Actually, streaming through your fingers is more accurate.

The subtle flow of Yang towards Yin explains why, when you're walking through the woods, you'll find your body naturally drawn down the slopes towards any running stream. This is a primal instinct that we have not lost just because we brought water indoors.

Many of the flaws in our modern buildings lie on the doorsteps of the male designer's addiction to the expression of Yang. Open vistas, overcharged with light, angular lines, great rooms, cathedral ceilings, make for a great visual impact in the slick, glossy, architectural magazines that are their barometer of success. Why? Because angles photograph easily and dramatically! These same qualities are what fail to nurture the human physiology.

There seems to be an inverse ratio between the size of the American bedroom and the sexual satisfaction enjoyed there. Many bedrooms frustrate couples romantically by being too bright and exposed, with too many windows, too much open space, exterior light invading the sanctuary, and an array of illuminated faces on radios, cable boxes, VCRs, and clocks. Besides this assault of visual light, the body has to contend with electrical magnetic fields associated with sockets and cords, not to forget the face of even a turned-off television. (Cover that big eye up when you are sleeping) The result is that the body never feels safe.

The pineal gland, which sets the body's clock, can only accomplish this at the darkest hour of the night, registered through closed eyelids. When a state of true darkness is never reached the clock doesn't set properly. The pineal gland is the ringmaster who announces the cascade of hormone reactions. When the ringmaster stutters it can result in a world of problems, not the least of which is a vanished sex drive. What's the real cause? An excess of Yang! Simply by darkening the windows, moving the bed away from the sockets, covering the extraneous light sources, or in other words, moving the space towards Yin, you will typically solve the problem. It's a lot easier to see a twinkle in your lover's eye in sparkling candlelight.

Not surprisingly, Yin is the area of retreat, since it recalls the body's memories of the womb, when we all breathed liquid for forty weeks and swam in the ocean human. Throughout the Bible, the Sutras, the Koran and other holy texts, the ideas of nurturing and divinity are always tied to the presence of water. Many of the early prophets were wanderers in the desert, so their very survival was linked to the cool springs and comforting shadows of the oasis.

In Asian Feng Shui, the association of water with money comes from their society's traditional source of wealth. The rice paddy. The Koku, Japan's standard of money for centuries, was based upon the amount of rice that would feed a family for a year. The connection between the color black and money comes from the cultural reality that when a rice farmer examines the roots of his plants, black soil had better be clinging to them. If the color is too light, then the soil is depleted of minerals, the plants won't thrive and the village will go hungry.

31

In Western cultures, the color black has long been associated with death and mourning, because in these countries they have traditionally been dry soil farmers. Black on the roots of the wheat means molds, cankers and crop failure. Yet even in the West, the most prized acreage has always been in the river valleys, where the winter floods nourish the land with mineral-rich, river silt. In the ecological system, as in the human body, the nutrients are transported by liquids. The prosperity of all life depends upon fluids. So significant is the power of Yin.

In explaining the differences of the polarities, don't confuse it with the contrast between healthy Chi and Sha, or disruptive energy. We're talking about completely different concepts. Yin and Yang are complete, healthy, archetypal forms that have real influence in our world. On the other hand, Chi signifies the intertwining of these two polarities, life in its completeness, the healthy organism with all of its requirements met, and a sense of cosmic identity. Sha is akin to electrical static; it is Chi that has been disrupted. In terms of modern science, Sha are molecules that have been damaged. In physiology, we call Sha "free radicals." It's an atom or a molecule that has lost electrons from its outer shell. In the bloodstream, they appear as barbed balls.

It's the damage they do as they scrape their way through the blood vessels that makes them so undesirable. In the environment, they are created when molecules are crushed and mashed or otherwise distorted. This happens inside the engines of cars and trucks, between the steel wheels and tracks of trains, in the pathway of deafening sirens. All of the things we think of as pollution are the free radicals of the natural world in which atoms are deformed and lose their identity. All of this are called Sha. If Chi is the breath of life, then Sha definitely needs a breath mint. So we didn't warn you about this technical bit, but it was too important for you to skip over.

When you use sweet-sounding chimes and beautiful colors, with rainbows cascading from crystals, you are pouring the antioxidants of creation over these damaged cells.

You help harmonize them and restore the electrons they lost, and help them rebuild their outer shells, to re-create their identities in a new, higher vibration form. You may use the light or sound pressure from mirrors and chimes to push the static away from important living spaces. After all, just because there's trash on the street, that doesn't mean you have to invite it in! Better that you should use an energetic broom to sweep it in another direction. Of course, sweep the Sha downhill or it will just find you again.

When juggling the flow of Yin and Yang, you're seeking a balance that suits the space, but that's different from stagnation. Yin slows down change by intermingling and stabilizing Yang. Yang revels in change but is invariably drawn to Yin. Energy needs to flow, but not too quickly, and setting the pace is the balancing of Yin and Yang. Keep in mind that in home and work place things that are Yang are bright, warm, active, dry, large, and fill up space. While things that are Yin are dark, cool, quiet, wet, small, and empty spaces.

A harmonious space brings harmony to your life.

Always remember that the energy flowing into your space from the outside world, from your own presence, from the furniture, the electronics, the plants, and the junk, (tasteful junk, we're sure), creates the music that you are going to dance to. You are constantly creating the song!

Chapter Four
The Bagua
The Map of Life
Where to Find Love and Money

A little note about the spelling of Bagua. It's a Chinese word and that language has a variety of major dialects. Because Chinese is a calligraphic language the word is not translated, it's transliterated. The sound is converted. Depending upon which dialect it's transliterated from the spelling will vary. Also it's actually two words. Our conversion to one word that's easy to pronounce is a convenient Americanization. Generally speaking when you find places where we vary from other commonly seen spellings or concepts, relax. Flexibility is important. We've made these adjustments to make it easy for our students. Take advantage of it.

The Bagua is the basic tool and philosophical instrument of Feng Shui. It's both a map and measuring device. By over laying the Bagua on the floor plan or visualizing its placement within a room, it allows us to divide any space into the various areas of life. These areas of life relate to the sequential stages of human experience. In simple terms, one section will indicate your wealth, and another will show your health. One area will show your friendships and another your romance. And on and on through the stages of experience we encounter in our Earthly journey.

One of the most fascinating things about the Bagua is that it works in two ways. We influence our environment and our environment influences us. So as you walk around the house considering the things you find in the sections marked out by the Bagua, you'll find them describing the story of your life. For example: If your love and romance section is of pile a sealed boxes, probably all of your fun is packed away and inaccessible. Using the Bagua will show the unique pattern of energy that you've painted on your environment. You can also use the Bagua from the other, proactive direction. By intentionally placing objects in the specific areas you want to change, you can improve those parts of your life. For another example: If you move those boxes out and place a nice love seat there, with a pair of heart pillows, or maybe a Teddy Bear couple, you'll upgrade your energetic program, and with that, improve your love life.

What we're presenting here is a ground-breaking approach to the Bagua. We take the relatively simple eight-part tool used by most Feng Shui practitioners and reveal it as a highly sophisticated and effective instrument for analyzing a current life situation and then quickly enacting change for the better. While the Bagua is a philosophical tool, it is also a precise and practical instrument for understanding and solving real issues. Coming down to Earth is what it takes to truly understand the workings of the Bagua! To begin with, we divide it into 12 parts because it better suits the needs of the modern world. We live in complicated times. Once again, relax. Yes this is different, and yet it is supported by ancient universal systems that are normally hidden behind the curtains of the mystery schools.

Once you get a good grip on the symbolism of the twelve sections, you'll understand the basic language of Feng Shui. You will also know how to draw all kinds of information from every room you enter. To set the stage it's helpful to consider the Chinese system, and repeat that Ba Gua simply means 8 trigrams. The Chinese esoteric traditions use multiples of 8. The trigrams are 3 line patterns that describe the passage of the year in the I Ching, or Book of Changes. There are 64 sequential trigrams, or 8 times 8 in the I Ching. The Chinese use 8 of those trigrams to delineate the directions of the compass: North, North-East, East, South-East, South, South-West, West, and North-West. In the Chinese tradition these 8 trigrams also symbolize the classic family: Mother, Father, 3 sons and 3 daughters.

These 8 characters relate to the 8 potential positions we take in life, that are expressed in 4 polarities:
• Strength and Receptiveness
• Arousing Movement and Gentle Insinuation
• Profound Intensity and Adaptability
• Patient Acceptance and Joyful Responsiveness

Warning, esoteric curves ahead, not for the philosophically faint of heart. These 8 qualities seem to align with the traditional descriptions of the Sun and Moon, 5 visible planets, plus Earth. This isn't surprising since the Chinese astrological systems are closely connected to Feng Shui. Their approach relies heavily upon the planets and stars. They focus less upon the astrological signs and geometrical relationships that Western systems use, probably because China's high incidence of earthquakes disrupts the taking of long term measurements that they require. We haven't read this anyplace else but the descriptions of the archetypes fit.

- Strength and Receptiveness
  (The Sun and the Moon)
- Arousing Movement and Gentle Insinuation
  (Jupiter and Venus)
- Profound Intensity and Adaptability
  (Saturn and Mars)
- Patient Acceptance and Joyful Responsiveness
  (Earth and Mercury)

Ch'ien, Creative, Father, SUN

K'un, Receptive, Mother. MOON

Chen, Arousing, 1st Son, JUPITER

Sun, Gentle, 1st Daughter, VENUS

K'an, Abysmal, 2nd Son, SATURN

Li, Clinging fire, 2nd Daughter, MARS

Ken, Keeping Still, 3rd Son, EARTH

Tui, Joyous, 3rd Daughter, MERCURY

The 8 Major Trigrams for the 8 Directions

This planetary connection is even more obvious when we look at the five stages, Metal, Water, Wood, Fire, and Earth. The confusion about this concept comes from two sources. First a mistranslation of the word stages as elements. Second the major omission of the qualities, Energy and Heat. These two vital components are well known in Chinese Medicine as being essential parts of the system. The difference between the stages and the qualities is that each stage prepares for the next, giving the impression that one changes into another. In reality the focus simply changes from one stage to another in the course of time. The qualities in contrast influence all equally, and are influenced equally. When the Chinese talk about Energy they describe the Heart energy, the Sun, which gives to all systems equally. When the heart is strong, everything is strong. When the heart is weak, everything is weak. Yet individual systems can be weak without substantially affecting the heart. When the Chinese talk about Heat they're talking about hormonal heat. The reproductive system pulls resources from all of the other systems. When all of the systems are strong then the Heat is hot. When the overall systems are weak or starved the Heat is cooled.

What is interesting is that while both Energy (the Sun) and Heat (Mars) are Yang in nature, Heat (Mars) is controlled by the Yin. This is a concept found in ancient Astrology where Mars, a masculine planet, is controlled by the feminine, the Yin. We can see this physically in the fact that while blood is red and clearly relates to the red planet Mars, it is controlled by the Veins, the Venous system (Venus), a player on the feminine team. In the following diagram the analogy is clear.

Even the design of the body is clear on the map. Metal (Mercury) controls the brain and the nervous system. Water (Moon) is on the left of the body, the receiving side, by the sodium (salt) rich stomach. Wood (Saturn) is also on the left side of the body, representing the structural system. Typically the left side of the body is bonier. Fire (Jupiter) is on the right of the body, the giving side, representing the muscular system, and the right thigh is often the most muscular part of the body. Earth (Venus) is on the right side, by the liver, the organ that must decide how to share and balance the resources traveling through the blood. Bringing us back to Metal (Mercury) who sometimes gives and sometimes takes. It has to serve both the Yin and the

Yang. Energy (the Sun) representing the heart is higher in the body, closer to the heavens, generous to all. Heat (Mars) is closer to the ground, receiving from all, condensing that vitality and passing it on into the generations.

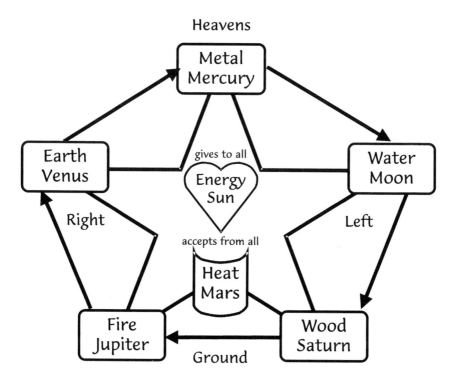

The 5 Stages and the 2 Qualities and their Planets

Yes, this is another place that we've completely leaped over the fences separating the mystery schools of major cultures. But these systems all describe the same natural and mystical phenomena. True, we've probably wandered into the deeper side of the pool, but we warned you up front. Maybe this will make the Chinese systems easier for you to understand, or maybe not. Either way we've put it into a western perspective so thanks for listening. End of warning zone.

In the Western tradition of measurement, the calendar,

the clock and the compass are subdivided into 12 parts and multiples of 12. These reflect the outer world and the 12 stages of the seasons as shown in the 12 months and the 12 signs of the zodiac. For a more complete description of the 12 signs of the zodiac and the planets see Chapter Ten, the Stars of Home.

The reasons for these differences are complex, technical, and philosophical, and if we explain any more of them here we're going to have to put more warning signs all over the place to protect the faint of heart. Let's just say that they arose out of the way that the building materials that were available to the cultures affected them philosophically. In other words, if one culture builds with bamboo and rice, while the other builds with stone and oak, their theories about the design of the natural world are going to be distinctly different. But stone, oak, rice, and bamboo are all creations of the Earth and Sky, so the same underlying principles apply. The two systems just subdivide space a little differently. By tapping into those deeper principles and defining the environment more exactly, we're able to employ this tool more effectively in a modern, Western-influenced world.

In the same way that the Bagua is the ancient Chinese philosopher's tool, when we look into western antiquity we find that the astrological Horoscope, or chart of the heavens, has fulfilled that role in the west. Beside the number of divisions each employs, the other difference is in their orientation. The Bagua is upside-down in relation to the Horoscope. Now we find this hysterical! Do you remember those cartoons of Bugs Bunny digging so deep in the Earth that he ended up standing upside-down in China? Guess what? Bugs was right! Why do we say that? Different parts of the Earth have different qualities. The Asian culture is Yin, small dark-haired people, insular societies, wet-soil

41

crops, with fertile lands cut by many rivers and prone to earthquakes. Western cultures are Yang, large people, light-colored hair, expansionistic, dry-soil crops on a very stable landmass.

In the Western Horoscope, the point most related to your career, or what you do, is at the top of the chart. In the Bagua, the career point is at the bottom. The top priority of the traditional Chinese culture was the family, the home, and whom you are descended from. The Chinese believe so strongly in the importance of the clan that the family name always comes first. This is the reverse of most modern Western Societies, in both philosophy and written form. In the West the family you are from may be important, but many famous people have become well-known under assumed names, with no connection to their original family. See what we mean, it's simple! Bugs was right!

When a Feng Shui practitioner arrives at a consultation, they'll take the Bagua and lay it over the floor plan of the building. To get the most personal, and emotional insight of the home, the practitioner aligns the Bagua with the front door, which is the public face of the building. To get a more cosmic and social perspective, they'll align the Bagua with the compass, and see how the building is aligned to the cosmic directions. The former method is easier, since even if you lose your compass, you can still usually find the front door. So if you're completely new to this we suggest you focus on aligning the Bagua with the entrance doors, and leave the compass for future study. To orient the Bagua on the floor plan you could make yourself a Bagua belt. Just take the diagram and staple it on to your belt so that when you walk into any room you'll know which section is where. Of course the easier, and less silly method, is to simply remember that when you walk into any room the far left-hand corner is money, and the far right-hand corner is love.

And to tell you the truth, that's most of what everyone is interested in.

In both methods, the house is segmented into multiple sections. Each of these sections has significance, and their condition tells the story of the household, and offers clues about where changes will be most effective. On the very personal basis the Bagua can be applied to any room, aligned with the principle door into that space. Be especially sensitive to the patterns in the bedroom and the office. Adjusting these rooms will often offer the most profound benefits for the residents.

The Me We Personal Bagua

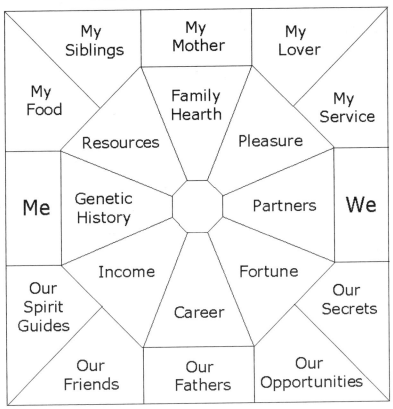

Align this Side of the Bagua with the Main Door Wall

The 8 Inner Sections is the Chinese System and the 12 Outer Sections are the Western System

Another primary difference between an 8 and 12 part system is the corners. The Chinese system rounds them off as if they are bending bamboo. The West divides the corners into two parts, one Yang, the other Yin. But we'll explain that as we go along. When we explain the significance of the 12 sections of the Bagua, we're going to use the 12 astrological signs; Aries, Taurus, Gemini, Cancer, Leo, Virgo, Libra, Scorpio, Sagittarius, Capricorn, Aquarius, and Pisces. These describe the cycles of the year and the stages of life, and are familiar to most westerners. So we're going to start in the east, section one, and work our way around the chart, explaining how the turning of time and the movement of Chi turns one thing into another in a continuous, graceful sequence.

The Bagua has four general areas, left and right, front and back. For simplicity's sake we're basing this upon the orientation from the entrance door of a single room. When you're standing in the doorway looking inside, the left is the area of the individual, and the right is the area of the couple. The back is the area of the home, and the front is the area of the community. For example, the far left-hand corner relates to issues of the personal resources. The near left-hand corner relates to issues of the public resources. The far-right hand corner relates to personal power. The near right-hand corner relates to issues of public power. This actually describes the traditional home. The formal rooms are towards the front and the kitchen and laundry are towards the back. The left and right polarity comes from the design of the human body. The primary Me organs are on the left side while the We organs are on the right. We hold a new baby over our left breast so their head is near the comforting sound of our heart, and we shake hands in greeting with the right hand.

Again and again we mention the importance of creating

a strong focus for the eye when you enter each room. Be aware of which section of the Bagua you're looking at first. That area is going to be the part of your life that you'll tend to concentrate on when you're there. Make sure that it's appropriate to what you want to accomplish.

Note: In the descriptions of the sections following we make references to the Astrological Signs and Planets. For a more detailed description of their qualities read the section on Location Charts in Chapter Ten.

Here are the parts of the Bagua. The sections follow a natural sequence analogous to the human life cycle. We include this analogy in our explanation as a helpful memory tool.

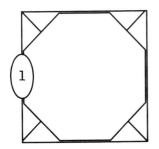

The First Section is the middle third of the left wall. This is the territory of courage, of the leap into consciousness, when you step over the threshold of life into birth. This is where the sprout bursts through the crust of the soil and the self discovers itself. The middle of the left-hand wall is the most central territory of the "Me". This is Springtime, and the red energy of Aries and Mars, the face and head. It is your physical constitution and bloodline. It is how you appear to others, as well as the raw power of your ego. It is the cry of the new-born baby. It is the Royal Me as the center of my world. This is dynamic Yang.

What do you have on this wall? What's on the floor? What is at chest height, and thus facing your heart? Does it make your heart sing? Does it represent how you see yourself? Choose this image well, because it's a portrait of how you see yourself. What is at eye level and above? Who are you planning on being when you arrive in the future?

Fill this area with images and objects that represent

healthy vitality. Independent, strong, dynamic themes should dominate here. In the home of a loving couple or family, it is wise to include a picture of the group to weave together the feeling of self-identity with that of belonging. Human images work best. Abstract art may not serve as well here, although plants do well as long as they are well rooted, enduring, and vital.

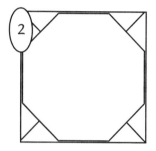

The Second Section is the far third of the left wall. Once the baby is born, what is their first concern? Food and love, and Mother's milk! Here we move from the concept of the Me to the idea of Mine. In life what is the next concern? Is the child nursing well, is the baby beautiful and strong? This area represents your essential talents, your personal beauty, your voice, and your willingness to be satisfied. Later in life it becomes the money you have in the bank, your real estate, and the wealth that you hold onto. This is the middle Spring time, the month of Taurus and Venus, when the leaves fill out the trees with soothing and sexy green. The crops in the fields reveal their promise, and the stability of the Earth is treasured. This is the region of the throat and shoulders. This is stable Yin.

Not surprising, plants have always been a favorite adjustment for this space, and they do provide that all-important stability. In the plants you will mirror the state of your resources. If you fill the area with low sitting, pot-bound, mature green friends, your resources may stabilize but not expand. If you hang young plants bursting with growth, over these foundation plantings, the Universe will happily expand your future financial horizons.

Be careful of any drains here. Buildings that suffer from a missing section, sewer pipes, or active vents in this area often turn into money pits. In Asia where the economy is

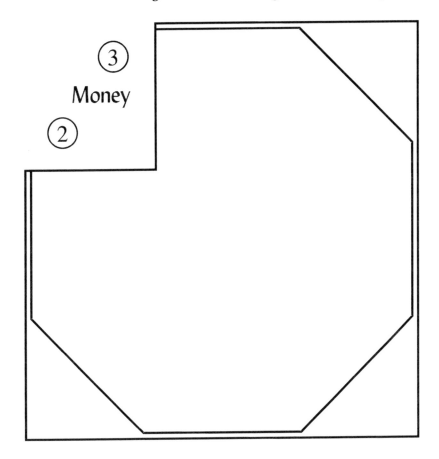

Watch Out for the Missing Money Section

based upon rice, a plant that likes its feet wet, people successfully place fountains in this section. However Western cultures are fed on dry-soil crops, and a fountain there often stimulates spending. Choose images that represent the bounties of the Earth, the rewards of love, and the beauty of nature.

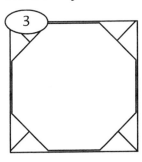

The Third Section is the left third of the back wall. Now the child develops speech and social connection with their siblings. The ability to reflect those around you becomes important. The talents are applied. The child develops mobility. This is where the child realizes that while they have a rattle, their sibling has a ball, so maybe they can make a deal. If the second section is the banker, the third section is the deal-maker. This is the time of Gemini and Mercury and the late spring when the insects become active. This is an area of communication among your intimates, as well as your local neighborhood. When you need to do some business or employ an agent of any kind, this is an area to activate. This is the area that shows your ability to find a common ground with other people, to demonstrate that you are like them. This is playful Yang.

The third section thrives on reflective materials, the written word, and anything that inspires the brilliant mind. It strongly influences the nervous system, and the arms and hands. Mirrors do great here, as do telephones, and mobiles with metal components. This is the money that's in the pocket, the ready cash for entertainment and daily concerns. If you want your communications to be clear, fun, and sparkling, then make sure that this area reflects those qualities.

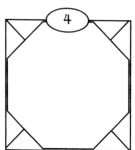

The Fourth Section is the middle third of the back wall. This is the area of the hearth and the warmth of Summertime. The Chinese call this "Rank" or "Fame" because in their society "Rank" was established by the core family into which you were born. Remember that the words "Fame" and "Family" are related. They even have the same first three letters. This is the point where the child becomes part of the family. In the cycle this is when their Mother says to them "Here honey, put this on the table," or " Do you want to help the other children shuck some corn for dinner?" Until then, the child isn't really a full fledged part of the heritage. They're more like baggage. (One of those beautiful Italian handbags of course) You carry them around. You carry their stuff around. But until they're able to participate in the communal family tasks, their photo isn't really secure on the mantle piece over the fireplace. And that is what belongs in this part of the house or room. Family pictures! In fact, when you move into a new home, if you immediately go to this section of the house and place a heavy piece of furniture there and cover it with the family pictures, you'll very quickly feel at home. On the other side of the coin, when you're ready to move, put those pictures away and put that heavy armoire on a mover's dolly. Energetically, when you do that you've pulled up anchor. This is the section of Cancer, the Moon and the early Summer when food becomes abundant. It relates strongly to the Mother and those who feed others. It affects the stomach and the breasts. It is nurturing Yin.

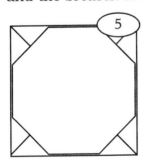

The Fifth Section is the right third of the back wall. This is the area of the heart, passion, and desire. This is where the child goes out into the local world and finds what they love doing, and whom they love doing it with. This is a very creative area, expressive, joyful, and passionate. When people complain about lack of love or fun in their lives, they should look here first. This is the time of Leo and the Sun, the high summer. Here's a point where the Western system diverges from the Asian, and from our experience, the Western is closer to the mark. At least for Westerners. this is the place of romance and affairs. It is the area of attraction but not of commitment. (Signing on the dotted line and showing up on the correct day at the church for the wedding is the province of the Seventh section) This is where we meet the love of our life, but we haven't convinced them to marry us yet. Let fun, nurturing and creativity, be found in this section, and make sure that there's room for two and it's cushy enough to be inviting. This is the beginning of the sections where we like to see things that are "TSSOS" (Twos, Same Species, Opposite Sex) This area really does affect the heart both physically and emotionally. It is passionate Yang.

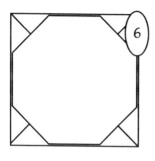

The Sixth Section is the far third of the right wall. This is where the convincing goes on. This is the area of practical love. This is late Summer and harvest time. This is Virgo and Mercury. The passion and creativity of the previous section are applied here. It relates to skills that we use in our daily lives. This is the area of apprenticeship and learning by example. In romance, it's the area of the engagement, and that's where we see the concept of virgin purity and perfectionism. That's the time to decide if our special love is Mr. or Mrs. Right. This is an extremely important area for health. Feeling both loved and useful is extremely important to good health. While the first section shows the inherent strengths, this area is the maintenance of health, hygiene, the cleanliness of the living environment, and personal grooming. This is why Mothers always tell their children to dress nice when they go out. So they look neat and clean and appeal to a prospective mate. After all, a part of a Mother's agenda is to get the kids married well. This area relates to the digestion and the autonomic nervous system. This is dutiful Yin.

Any kind of artistic or craft tool or musical instrument resides here happily. Herbs and nutritional supplements also fit cozily into this part of the corner. Be careful to keep this spot clutter-free and organized, since it has a subtle influence over the efficiency and organization of the entire space.

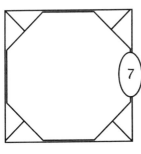

The Seventh Section is the middle third of the right wall. This is where we show up at the courthouse and sign on the dotted line. This is where we walk down the aisle to take the vows of partnership. This is where you extend your right hand and shake on the deal. This is committed partnership and marriage. It is the transition into the social We, with all of the formality and scrupulous attention to fairness. This is the area of Libra and Venus. The Chinese refer to this area as relating to children, because from their social viewpoint marriage is not as important to the individual as it is to the whole family. In the past it was not unusual for a successful Chinese man to have more than one wife and several concubines. We tend to frown on that practice here in the West. This is the area that denoted their most-binding marriage, namely, the one that produced the legal heir. Here's the difference between sections five and seven, five is passion and seven commitment. In the modern western world, we tend to feel that the person you love and feel passionate about is the same person you are suppose to be committed to. It relates to the hips, the balancing point of the body. This is equitable Yang.

For the sake of good relationships, we like to suggest that any objects or images here have some quality of pairs. Or as we're fond of saying, pictures of TSSOS. To offer no offense to same-sex couples, what we're looking for here is a sense of polarity. Place images here that represent what you want your partnerships to be about. Avoid fantasy unless that's what you want for your relationships. Avoid pictures of Angels here, because if Angels are having sex, they're not telling anyone. Aim for balance, structure, and harmony.

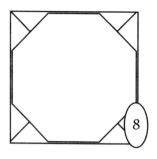

The Eighth Section is the near third of the right wall. Once you form the partnership what's the first challenge? Sharing power, and that's what this area is about. In marriage the first issues are about sex and sharing the checkbook. In business partnerships, the issues are about the control and the distribution of benefits. This area resonates with a powerfully emotional and transformational energy that's inclined to risk-taking. The eighth section is one of the most hidden and misunderstood areas of life and often when we look in people's spaces there's nothing there. That's not surprising, since this is the area of Scorpio and Mars/Pluto, and it relates to the extreme beauty and danger of the desert, and those energies that often act behind closed doors. This is the sexuality of the married couple. It relates to the sexual organs and the adrenal glands. It is the business dealings of associates. It is the political leverage that manipulates from behind the scenes. This is seductive Yin.

The paintings of Georgia O'Keefe, both her desert scenes and her luscious, sensual flowers fit here hand in glove. This is an area of extremes. Images of power, cooperative venture, commitment in action, mountaintops, and the kinds of challenges that require the help of your peers to accomplish. A team of climbers scaling a cliff is an appropriate image. On the other hand, an image that is deeply and beautifully sensual also resonates comfortably here.

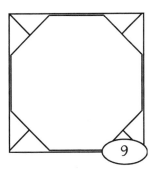

The Ninth Section is the right third of the front wall. Once you scale the heights, what do you get? A great view! After you've braved the ocean crossing, what do you get? A better understanding of the world! If the Third Section is where you learn your native language, the Ninth is where you learn foreign languages. They may be professional languages, the arcane words of medicine, law, and philosophy. They can also be the arcane theories of physics and science or the specialized instruments of finance and trade. This is the area of expanding horizons, travel, distant lands, philosophy, and higher education. It relates to the thighs and to the body's ability to stretch.

In practical terms, once you've gained the leverage and power of the Eighth Section, you use it to extend your reach. Whether it's through getting an appointment to an institute of higher learning for your child, or trading visas for your business. This is the area of Sagittarius and Jupiter. Remember that the archer is a Centaur who loves to leap and hit distant targets. Jupiter is the largest planet and covers his territory in a mix of gallop and saunter. So this area relates to the way that you extend your reach into the outer world. Here we've entered that critical area along the wall where the main door to the building or room is located. Doorways in this part of the wall tilt the energy toward education and consulting. This is one of the prime areas to activate for any kind of real estate sale because it promotes optimism and looking to the future. This is the area of what you know. This is adventurous Yang.

Place things here about the future you wish to create, and by that we mean the future in the outside, social world. If you find that you're traveling too much, then anchor this area with something heavy and difficult to move. If you need good advice, put images here that represent wisdom to you.

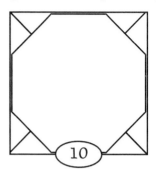

The Tenth Section is the middle third of the front wall. Once you've traveled and studied, the time comes to get to work and climb that ladder of success. This is the area of Capricorn and Saturn. This is where we seek the recognition of our peers. The schoolbooks and backpack of the Ninth Section are put away. With the Tenth Section comes the business attire, and dry cleaning bills. This is a formal area, concerned with the rules and regulations and opinions of others. As befits a section of the space where we often find the front door, it relates to your efforts in the outside world as well as to reputation. This is the area of "How you are known". When you feel that you're not getting recognition for your efforts, this is the place to look. When you don't use the front door and instead sneak in through the side or back entrances, this area goes inactive, together with those parts of your life. If the front door is actually here, make sure it's grand and attracts attention both inside and out. This enhances your reputation and insures the hierarchy of the family, enforcing order in the house. This is responsible Yin.

This is a good spot for that grandfather clock or an equally imposing structure. This area relates to the knees and the bones, so its not surprising to find things here that are strong and rigid, such as a picture of a great building. In fact, if you are having a problem with discipline or responsibility, it may be that whatever you have placed here is not creating a strong enough message. When the door is located here, it tunes the house towards taking care of responsibilities, conservative thinking, and attention to public opinion. This is the strong woman beside the successful man. This is the top of the grandest tree in the forest.

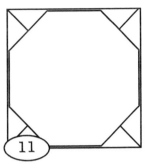

The Eleventh Section is the left third of the front wall. Once your reputation has been established you get to reap the rewards. While Sections Two and Three relate to the money you hold on to, either in the bank or in your pocket, Section Eleven is where new money enters your realm. This is the area of "Who you know", and as anyone who's been in business will tell you, It's not what you know but who you know that makes you money. Why else did you spend so much time developing that reputation if it wasn't to attract opportunities? This is the area of Aquarius and Saturn/Uranus. It is the area of innovation and that is one of the keys to success. In other words, those who adjust to change first, win.

If you feel that your connections to your community and friends are getting stale, liven up this area with something unusual. Together with Section Twelve, these are the best places for abstract paintings. Images of groups of people also work well here. If you fill this section with ultraconservative furniture or antiques that are no longer in daily service, you may find yourself being viewed as professionally old school or even outdated. Innovate! This area relates to the shins and the inner parts of the aura. This is innovative Yang.

In many homes, this section is the formal dining or living room that is rarely used. The result is an income that is stable and unexciting. In these cases, we'll suggest putting interesting glass pieces in the windows so they can be seen and enjoyed by people passing by. It is also a way to gather in that energy. Decorating this room in a playful and slightly outlandish, eclectic, or experimental way sparks that streak of creativity that is part of being a truly successful human being.

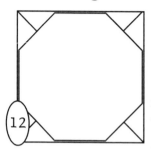

The Twelfth Section is the near third of the left wall. Once you've climbed the ladder of success and earned all that money, what do you do next? Buy your way into heaven! Whether that heaven involves a sailboat cruising off to far horizons, compassionate contributions and actions, meditation and spiritual communion, restrictions and denial of the ego, or the haven of the artist, they all involve going beyond the self, onward to a connection with the divine. This is one of the hidden sections, together with the Eighth, and these are the areas to investigate when you feel there are hidden forces at work in your life. In South America, these are the places we look at when we're asked questions about curses and voodoo. Because of their positioning in the room they spend more time being seen with the corners of the eyes than any other sections. This is the area of the eye ruled by the autonomic nervous system, so they are the most beyond the control of the conscious mind. This is the area of Pisces and Jupiter/Neptune. This is where you leave the world behind and dissolve into the Universal Spirit. That process could take place in a church or a wine bottle, through the heights of inspiration or the valleys of despair. These are the fish swimming beneath the surface, elusive, shimmering, and beautiful. This is devoted Yin.

It is the place where things get lost and forgotten, so it becomes especially important to keep this area clean and orderly (A mighty challenge for this section). This is the area for an altar, the studio, or the meditation space. It is the place of dreams and dreaming, so be careful that the things you put there lend themselves to that pursuit. Inspirational themes prevent the dissolving aspects from taking hold.

So here you have the map of space on a horizontal plane, but just as the body has different sections related to height, so does the room. The lower part of the wall has to do with the past or the foundation of your life. The middle part of the wall reflects the current moment and needs. The upper part of the wall shows your plans for the future. When we divide the 12 vertical parts by these 3 horizontal planes, we have 36 distinct sections. Now consider that each of these 36 parts has a Yang element and a Yin element, so by adding this additional polarity we can further divide the space into 72 parts. In the esoteric tradition, 72 is the number of the Goddess, because 72 degrees is the angle that divides the circle into a five-pointed star. Seventy-two degrees is also the angle that forms the ends of the Vesica Piscis, the fish shape that represents the creativity of Mother Earth. The circle, the line, and the Vesica Piscis are the starting point in the construction of any building based upon sacred geometry. It's all an expression of the Divine pattern of the cosmic fabric within which we live.

Don't look so worried. There are plenty of changes you can make in your life using the 12 basic parts. The concepts of past (low), present (middle), and future (high) make the transition to 36 parts an easy one. As far as the 72 divisions, let's not get crazy now. Just be aware that each part contains a Yang and Yin component. The Yang part initiates, and the Yin part reacts. The Yang fills up, and the Yin dispenses. Yang begins, and Yin completes. Remember that in Feng Shui it's often a good idea to save the philosophizing until after you've moved the furniture.

A Guide to the Bagua Maps

The Bagua is a very interesting and useful tool for understanding how environments shape the energy that creates your reality. This section is meant to illuminate its workings in greater detail. It's helpful to understand that the Bagua can function on multiple levels. It can be adapted to a variety of situations. It is most often used to understand three important, interrelated energy systems, Earth, Human and Celestial. In other words, are you using the Bagua to understand the physical Earth Energy System, and aligning it to magnetic north? Are you applying it to the emotional Human Energy System and aligning the Bagua to the doorway? (This is the easiest system to learn and the best place to start.) Or are you applying it to the Mental/ Spiritual/Celestial Energy System and aligning the Bagua to celestial north?

Even when taking the simplest approach, the Bagua can seem to be as complicated as life itself. To help you understand the Bagua easily, we have separated the main concepts into a progressive series of separate maps, each dealing with another essential facet of the system. This is very much like Cartographers create individual charts focusing on state lines, topography, highways, demographics or climate, etc.

There are a number of different Bagua that have been popular in different eras, depending upon the school that was currently in vogue. These differences were based on the prevailing cultural tilt and the varied locations on the Earth of the cities where Feng Shui was practiced. These philosophical differences were normally expressed in the arrangement of the trigrams. The 8 icons, each made up of a variation of 3 solid or broken lines, which form the foundation of the I Ching.

The only problem with tossing around trigrams is that most Westerners don't have a strong cultural connection to them. Setting out to decipher them and to understand the reasons for the variations will lead you in a fascinating and circuitous route that won't necessarily get you any closer to understanding the workings of the Bagua in practice. In the name of clarity, we have purposely limited the use of confusing symbols, including the trigrams. We have also chosen definitions for the Bagua sections that are more tuned to a modern, western culture.

Maps 1 through 6 are aligned with the front door of the building or the main door to a room. This application works through the projection of the pattern of the human aura upon the space. It's the most detailed, emotional and immediate system and its influence extends throughout the social life. Maps 5 and 6 demonstrate how to use this Bagua with a building or room.

Note: as we move into the Bagua maps that are aligned with the cardinal directions, please note that they appear upside down in relation to the western custom of placing north at the top. Why? Bugs Bunny was right! So as it's noted on the maps, south is up, north is down, east is left and west is right.

Map 7 is a special case. This Bagua is aligned to magnetic north, and it shows our relationship with the flow of magnetic energy across the face of the Earth. This is where dowsing rods come in handy because there are conduits of various kinds of energy that flow in the ground beneath our feet. It's a very physical and practical Bagua. For most people this will have the least number of applications. It has the smallest sphere of influence around us but size in this case does not equate to power. These forces can be very strong. It can have a great influence over the health and attitude of the individual. The interpretations for this Bagua may seem simple. That's because it's describing a very basic energy. We've presented it here to demonstrate the differences between the magnetic and celestial orientations.

Maps 8 and 9 relate to our relationship with the Mental/Spiritual/Celestial energies. This is aligned with the true cardinal directions and true celestial north. In most places in the world this is different from magnetic north. This represents a modern form of the compass Bagua. In Tango, we've avoided touching on the traditional Compass Bagua or Loupan, which is potentially one of the most confusing schools of Feng Shui. This is true in part because of the difference between magnetic and celestial north. This means that the compass systems must be precisely aligned for differing locations. Also there are certain astronomical precessions that have taken place over the ages that need to be considered in order to use the Loupan accurately. So what we offer here is a very modern, western version that hopefully, will be easier to use. Map 9 shows an example of applying the celestial Bagua to a house.

The knowledge offered by directions is very powerful. But bringing traditional compass concepts into the mix along with the personal, door aligned Bagua system tends to confuse people. We'd rather avoid that. We suggest that you start with the door-aligned Bagua and after you feel comfortable with that, explore the other systems of alignments. Just remember that it's not that one system is right and another wrong, they simply have different applications.

By getting familiar with the language of directions presented in Chapter 9, The Powers of the Earth, you'll get a sense of how the compass works in a practical sense. By taking a walk through Chapter 10, The Stars of Home, you'll start getting a feel for how directions and archetypes fit together on a philosophical level. There are all kinds of remarkable things you can do with modern Compass Feng Shui once you understand it. This will give you a start. We plan on covering compass systems in greater detail in later books.

Map 10 shows the relationship between the western astrological signs and the sections of the Bagua. This is very helpful since it puts this system into a western symbology. Another little side note; we considered also showing how the Bagua relates to the Chinese horoscope, however that would have meant moving into a detailed explanation of the transits of Jupiter and Saturn, the difference between tropical and sidereal zodiacs and the secrets of the Imperial Astrologers. Then we'd have to post Danger Ahead signs all over the place. We decided to save that for another day.

Later on in Chapter 10 you'll see a western astrological chart which is a modern variant of these ancient systems. You'll also see a Location Chart there. This is something of a missing link between the Bagua and that modern astrological chart. It's not critical that you understand the connections in order to use the Bagua or directions effectively but it's fun to see how these ideas have evolved.

No matter how you view the Bagua, it's important to maintain some real mental flexibility. What we're portraying here, complex as it seems, is only the tip of the iceberg. Remember that polarities shift with the passage of night and day. Change is the only constant and whether you intend to focus on your spiritual, emotional or physical needs can determine the way in which you use the Bagua and which reference point you align it with.

Please review these maps many times as you learn to apply and refine your use of the Bagua. There is a complex interplay of concepts presented here. As you touch upon them over time, you'll find that they unlock many puzzles about how your relationship with your environment works and how you can improve that exchange.

Let's start by looking at the Bagua from our personal perspective, in other words, in relationship to me and mine. To make it easy to use, let's align the Bagua with the main doorways to either a building or room. The inner 8 divisions show modern definitions for the traditional Asian meanings of the 8 parts of the Bagua. The outer 12 sections show the more complex Western interpretations for these areas.

The Me We Personal Bagua

Align this Side of the Bagua with the Main Door Wall

This is the Bagua that shows the changing Universe and expresses Yin and Yang in a continuous clockwise cycle. Often when someone has difficulty producing the correct results when using the Bagua, it's due to not understanding that the corners contain both Yin and Yang parts. Before you start making your changes, you need to decide whether that part of your life requires the activation of the Yang or the Yin in order to achieve the results you desire.

The Nature of Yin and Yang in the Bagua

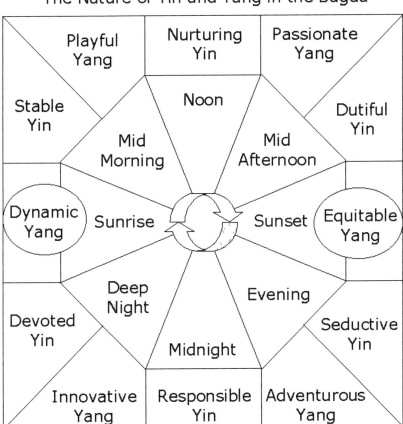

Align this Side of the Bagua with the Main Door Wall

When the Bagua is aligned with the main door it relates it intimately to the personal life. We can assign all kinds of things to its sections. For instance, which part of the Bagua relates to small electrical appliances? You're not sure? Don't feel bad, it's a trick question. It depends upon whether they're for personal use or professional use. The former is section 3, while the latter is section 6. So let's consider the Bagua in greater detail.

Deeper Meanings of the Personal Bagua Sections

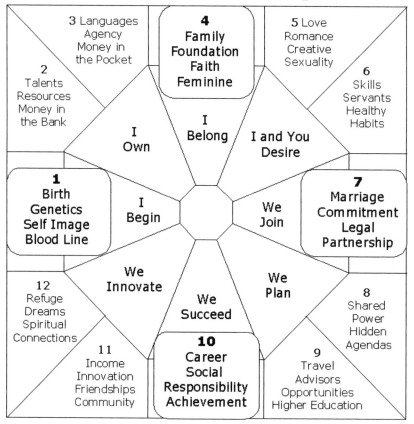

Align this Side of the Bagua with the Main Door Wall

The position of the door is always important. Whether a doorway is to either side or in the center of the entrance wall establishes a primary energetic program related to how you relate to the social world. Let's look at how different doorways program a building or room.

The Meanings of the Three Doorways

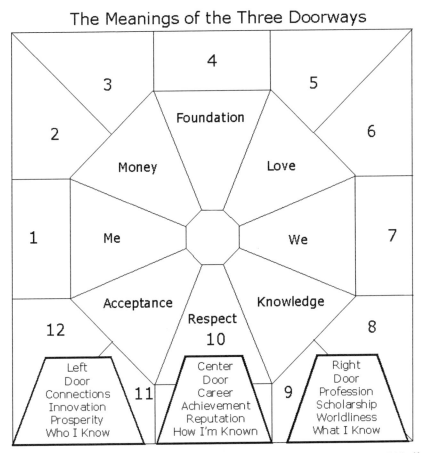

Align this Side of the Bagua with the Main Door Wall

When you lay the Bagua over the entire property or building you get an idea of the overriding program. Very simply, align the bottom of the Bagua, sections 9,10 and 11, along the wall where you find the front door. That door will be situated in one of those three sections. From that overall footprint, you can now determine where the basic sections are and also if there are any missing or extended areas. This gives you a sense of the volume and topography of the energy systems that the building is holding and shaping.

How to Place the Bagua Over the Whole Building's Floor Plan

Align this Bagua with the Building's Front Door

Applying the Bagua to an individual room is very simple. Align the bottom of the Bagua, sections 9, 10 and 11 along the wall where you find the main door. The far left-hand corner is Money and the far right-hand corner is Love. Look at the contents of the room in detail, and don't forget that relative height is significant. The lower third of the wall is the past, the middle third of the wall is the present and the upper third of the wall is the future.

How to Place the Bagua Over the Individual Room

This Bagua is Aligned Based Using the Rooms Main Door

Warning, Falling Rocks Ahead. This Bagua is Aligned with Magnetic North and it has very limited applications. We're including it here to help clarify the differences between aligning the Bagua with magnetic north or aligning the Bagua with celestial or true north. This Magnetic Bagua reveals how the physical body is affected by the magnetic flows of the Earth and how they influence the physical health. Don't try to find a strong correlation between the magnetic and celestial Bagua because they're as different as night and day. This Bagua will show you how the pattern of your aura interacts with the magnetism of the Earth. Aligning these two offers wonderful benefits for your health.

The Bagua Aligned with Magnetic North

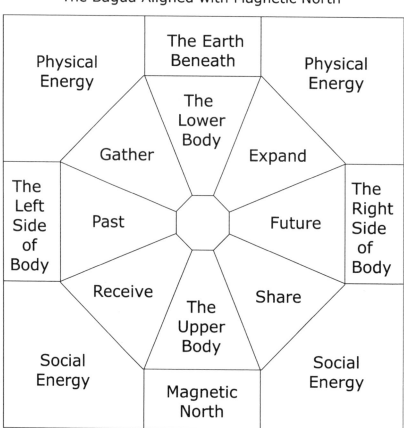

Align This Side With Magnetic North

When you align the Bagua with the Compass Directions, you're working with the highest expressions of Chi. Activating a direction draws that energy to you. This shows not only the influence of the planetary bodies upon the space but also the quality of light that daily bathes your environment.

The Meanings of the True Compass Directions

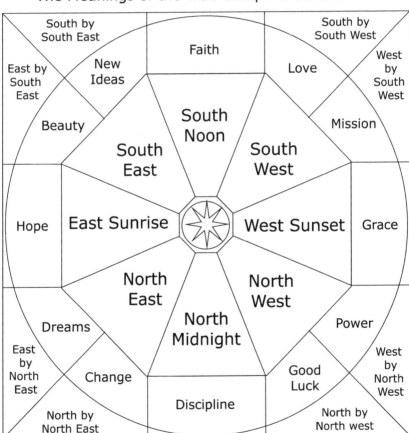

Align This Side With Celestial North

The way in which the building is aligned with the true directions and thus the celestial energies, reveals the higher purposes of that building's program. This is also true in the macrocosm and microcosm, for properties and desks. Remember that true North is the direction with which maps are aligned. So if you're not sure which way your building is facing, check a detailed map.

How to Overlay the Compass on an Existing House

Align This Side With Celestial North

Here is the western astrological correlation to the Bagua. These definitions can be very helpful since they put the Asian concepts into a western framework. The actions of the astrological energy systems are evident in all forms of the Bagua. The primary archetype continues to function at all levels. This is because it's a projection of the complex engine of the planets that drives life forward and creates the concept of time as we know it. That's probably a pretty profound philosophical point and we've tried to avoid excessive philosophy in favor of practicality, but sometimes it sneaks in.

How the Astrological Signs Relate to the Bagua

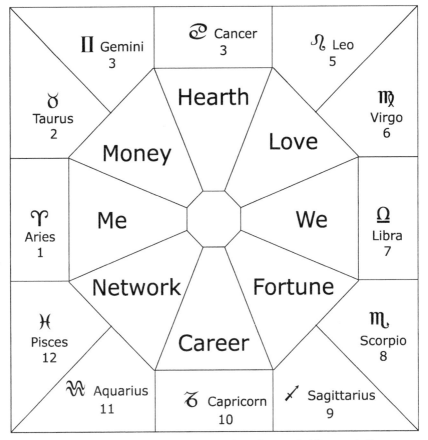

This Correlates to the Door and Celestial Aligned Baguas

Chapter Five
Immediate Solutions
Quick Fixes & Almost Instant Cures

In action, Feng Shui is less mysterious and more practical than you might think. It's down to Earth, logical, and often obvious. For example, if your electrical cords are a tangled knot, your life is probably all tangled up too. If you can't keep your energy straight, how will you be able to keep your life straight? The effects of such relatively simple solutions are quite remarkable. When you straighten out the cords, the knots in your life start to magically relax!

Remember that everything is energy. Electrical appliances, sockets, and wires have fields emanating from them, even when they're turned off. Tangled cords send out torturous vibrations. These chaotic fields have a damaging effect on the people and animals living around them. Not only that, when your body continually sees and feels chaos, you create chaos in other areas of your life. We are very literal animals. What we see is what we create!

Look for your cluttered or neglected corners and where they fall in the personal Bagua. They offer clear road signs pointing out the neglected areas in your life. Clutter is often trapped fear. The Chi is stuck! Subsequent areas of the Bagua are now starved for energy by the logjam upstream. By contrast, empty areas don't hold onto the energy. The Chi may whiz by and slam into the next area, totally forgetting the first, and throwing your life out of balance. People who have all their things along one side of the room are denying some part of their life. Everything affects everything! If any part of your life is stagnant, check for cluttered corners and clean them out. If something is missing in your life, check out the empty spots. You may see the same pattern emerge with the same sections of the Bagua in each room overburdened or neglected. Why? Because you're painting the same pattern again and again wherever you go.

Oftentimes in a family where the primary nurturer is overwhelmed (usually, but not always the Mother) the far right-hand corner, the nurturing area, will be piled high with all the extra debris.

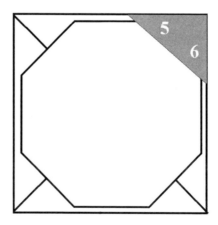

When the Nurturing Sections are Clogged

In a bedroom of a teenage boy, this is where you'll find a giant pile of dirty laundry. After all, at that age, Mom is basically the source for clean laundry, which equates to nurturing in their dictionary. Want to take bets on how many other nurturing corners in this house would also be overburdened along with the nurturer?

The opposite side of the coin is not any more appealing. We have been on more than one consultation where we have found clutter everywhere...except in the resource sections, Sections 2 & 3.

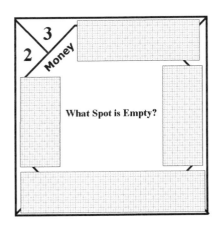

Curiouser and curiouser, Alice! This corner would be strangely and blatantly neglected. In our foolish youth we would accept a check from these clients, which of course, bounced to Zanzibar! Why? These clients weren't foolhardy enough to incur the wrath of the Feng Shui Wizards. No, they had simply neglected to make a deposit; they lost touch with their resources! Poetic, isn't it? When we find an empty money corner now, we immediately say, "Cash, No checks, please!"

Eeek, Clutter Alert! Where did all this junk come from anyway? How do you get rid of clutter effectively? First off, invite a friend or relative over to help. Someone that has no problem cutting to the chase and eliminating that wonderful piece of gimcrack that you may someday find the perfect spot for. Into the trash with it! Next case! Even if you decide to go it alone, the first thing that you want to do is hang something large and bright red (a raincoat, a slinky dress) where you can't help but see it from the entrance to that

closet, room, garage, or whatever. This will elevate your
energy so that you'll be up to the task at hand. Red
activates everything, which is the reason that stores and
restaurants use it so effectively to get you to eat, spend,
shop, and so on. Next, you want to start from the entrance.
Don't try to dig yourself out from a corner. That strategy
only leads to madness.

The fastest way to
produce clutter is to
store something behind
the door, so make sure
that doorways are
completely unblocked.
Get the shoe bag, coat
hook, or vacuum cleaner
out from behind the
door! This lets in the full
breath of Chi, instead of
the bare trickle that
led to it becoming

*A Cabinet behind the door is Clutter
Waiting to Happen*

stagnant, or in
other words
cluttered, in the
first place. When you clear the path, you'll have help from
the natural flow of the Universe to get things moving. Follow
the energetic path and work in the same clockwise direction.
The more you open up the pathway for energy, the more
energy it will give you. The added benefit is that you can
simply back out the door whenever you need a break. You
don't become trapped by the vines that have turned the
room into a jungle.

Beware of dripping faucets. Keep in mind that in Asian
Feng Shui, water is representative of money so dripping
water is more than the loss of the cost of the water itself.

You will find that you can never hold onto money for very long. No matter how much comes in, it just slips through your fingers! If money is a concern, leaks are a priority. The Chinese relate water to money

because the basis for their economy is rice, a water-grown crop. The Western feeling about water is more nebulous and problematic. In Western homes water is primarily something that drains away. We have to be careful about the location of drains. Watch out for bathrooms in Sections Two, Three and Seven, the areas of resources and partnerships. Keep those fixtures in top condition and you'll be able to control the rate of speed with which your resources flow out. If you want your books to balance, balance the Yin and the Yang, the wet and the dry dynamics of your resource areas.

Of course, if you just can't handle another dime in the bank, don't activate your resource sections and don't change a thing in Sections 2 (money in the bank), 3 (money in the pocket) and 11 (money coming in the door). Don't put any little plants in there to grow big and leafy. Don't put a nice chime, sun catcher, or crystal in there to keep the area active. Yea, just leave it empty and sparse. A little hint, if you have a bathroom in one of these money areas, the best thing to do is to make it so bright and beautiful, that your friends want to camp out in it. This goes the same for kitchens in these areas. Make the energy levels so high that those little drains in the sinks and fixtures are no competition.

Of course, if we come by for a consultation, don't be surprised when we ask for cash. Seriously! Be aware of what you put in the resource section. No bonsai trees! Think about it. You actually stunt its growth and it takes hundreds of years to accomplish the final result. Just how patient are you anyway? On the other hand, if you have a large plant that is pot-bound, the Universal energy looks at it and says, "Hmm, no more room for growth in the wealth section; they must have enough." You want stable resources but tuck some plants around it that are small, fast-growing and impossible to kill, like Spider plants, Golden Pathos, Wandering Jews, or Ivy. If there is storage in that area, make sure that it's orderly and useful. If you can't use live plants in this area, you might employ other symbols of prosperity and growth such as golden, expensive-looking objects, photos, or images of your dream house in the mountains. Avoid pictures that are abstract, nebulous, or ethereal. One caveat to that: The number 11 section loves abstract art and eccentric and innovative images and gadgets.

When you move things around, things change. If your life is great and you don't want it to change, then don't go moving things. Look for clues in your environment about your willingness to face changes in your life. We had a client who clearly wanted to stop time. She had a collection of antique watches, all stopped. Her calendars were all months out of date, and almost every mirror in the house was crazed and stained. She had suffered from anxiety attacks for years, and this was her reaction. She wanted time to stand still. Keep your mirrors clear, clocks set, and calendars up to date if you want to live in the present and face towards the future.

Let's talk about those squeaky and sticking doors.

They are the area where energy from one space is translated into another. Why do they squeak and get out of kilter? Because what's the most important tool for communication after the voice? The hands! We point, we type, and we write. Well, the tension people feel is expressed through their hands. When they are stressed, they push harder on the doorknobs, which rubs the oil off the hinges. After a while, all that pressure will pull the screws out of the jams and the door starts to stick. When doors squeak, it's like hearing mice. This is a sound our bodies dislike. This creates more stress. When doors stick, communication is stuck, and important things go unspoken. If you want to be heard and understood, fix those doors! Usually teenagers' doors stick or squeak. Pretty symbolic, don't you think?

When you have kids in the house, always keep that oilcan close by. At the first sign of a squeak, get to work. In businesses where communications are intense and complex, squeaky doors often show up. After all, if people are always pressed to make their point, teach, and explain, the channels of communication become strained, and so they need a little grease. Think of using oilcans as promoting good manners, which are after all, the lubrication that makes social interaction pleasant and workable. A little note: We use olive oil right from the kitchen, it smells nice and it has a great energy.

Problems with the exterior doors reveal difficulties in dealing with the social world. This might mean problems with neighbors or people at work, or even the government. When the interior doors are malfunctioning, it means the communication problems are cropping up inside in the daily interactions. If you're not communicating well with your spouse or if the kids aren't listening, oil those interior doors.

Spaces that are too "Zen", sparse or bare can make for boring lives. It's important to remind yourself that you are connected. At work, it's nice to have pictures of loved ones where you can see them. It reminds you about why you go to work. Write affirmations like "I am wonderful, I am healthy, I am full of vitality, I am worthy of love, I am on track to be a millionaire." Post them so you see them every day. This pushes you in the right direction. Remember that saying: "What you see is what you get," really is "What you see is what you do!" It's those personal objects that humanize an impersonal environment. We always travel with a chime that hangs on our hotel room door, so when we enter we hear the sounds of home. It makes all the difference to us.

Bells or chimes on the inside of exterior doors create no less than magic in a home with children. doors represent the adults in the home because they're the ones who control the keys. A bell that rings when the door is opened gets the child's or employee's attention, putting the idea of the parent or boss (same thing, right?) inside their head! Chimes are placed on the inside of any exterior door, with the largest chime reserved for the front door as viewed from the street. When it sings, it's the voice of responsibility and a reminder that consequences follow after actions, like that issue about wiping their feet on the mat before running through the house.

Just as exterior doors represent the parents, windows represent the children.

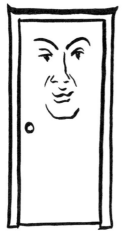

If the windows outnumber the doors, especially if the windows are uncovered and dominate a space, the children run the parents even if they have long grown and moved out! Want to know why?

Reflective surfaces bounce energy around your space. The reflectivity of the windows heightens communication levels. Kids are generally noisier and smaller. The reflectivity projects the child's mental aura onto the parent's heart chakra. It gives the little one a direct path to the parent's heart. Once that pattern is there its difficult to dislodge. Remember the saying: "Children should be seen and not heard." Well, when builders started putting more windows into our houses at the end of the Victorian era, that concept flew out the window. Exterior doors are the routes to the "real" world. When the chaos inside overwhelms them, the parents and bosses spend all their time looking in rather than out. Their focus becomes crisis management rather than future planning. Ideally, three to four windows per exterior door are a manageable number. If the kids are out of control hang more curtains, and put a chime on every exterior door.

Chimes on the door and in the yard also work as a security alarm. Their resonance creates a protective field in the home's vicinity. Everyone who passes by and hears the chime thinks to themselves: "Ah, there's someone there!" The energy level by the entrances is kept high preventing negativity and stagnation from accumulating.

81

So don't forget to take that small chime along when you travel and hang it on your hotel room door! What good Feng Shui! While you're at it, pack a small refracting crystal (A rainbow maker) to transform the energy in the room as well. You never know when you will get a hotel room with the dreaded western light! Americans frown on the Asian practice of painting the western-facing windows black, so you need to put color back into the harsh, white light that comes from the west. That's how to travel with rainbows!

Here's how you deal with the neighbor's barking dogs or any offensive noises or sight outside your home. Put small mirrors in the windows facing the dogs. They will reflect the noise back, and the owners will really hear it for the first time and take the dogs inside. Mind you, they bring the dogs inside because the barking annoys them. They're not worried about you, but whatever works. We know from first-hand experience. In fact, not only did our mirrors reflect back the noise, they reflected back the ugly yard which was promptly cleaned up prior to fresh sod being laid down. Just a little Feng Shui magic! Here's the inside techno-scoop. What do the mirrors reflect back to your unconscious neighbor? Light pressure. Photons. Information! Don't they use fiber-optic cable to transmit your phone conversation? When you put up a mirror against an offending sight, you are creating an energy loop, playing back the message you receive to the people who are sending it to you.

This also works well for keeping your property safe from vandals. The light pressure coming from the mirrors gives the impression of someone watching; that mysterious sensation we have all felt at one time or another, when we just know someone is watching us. What we're feeling is the light pressure from the other person's eyes. All of the accumulated energy of their brain and nervous system is running through their eyes. It's not surprising you would feel it.

Here's a hint from Cupid. To unify a couple or family, select a symbolic object with two or more pieces. One person (that would be you) sleeps with these objects under your pillow for 3 days to infuse them with the unifying influence. Then place the pieces by the bed or work place of each person. This can be voluntary, where you offer it to them in the spirit of togetherness, or if they don't share your altruistic hopes, tuck the object under their mattress or in their favorite chair. If they are going to zone out in front of the tube, they are in that ideal mode to reap the benefits of your behavior-modification techniques. Just remember: Do it with love. A couple of suggestions: Take a necklace that can be separated or use matched pieces of rose quartz. This lovely pink, natural crystal is well known for its calming and loving vibration. Pieces of rose quartz can sit on the respective nightstands of the couple to promote relaxation, affection, and happy dreams. Carry them with you when you travel to feel connected even while you are apart.

The Feng Shui Tool Box

What Have You Got to Work With?

There are a variety of tools at your disposal to correct all of your Feng Shui faux pas. We've listed a few of our own favorites here, although the only limit is your imagination. What qualifies them as tools is that they manipulate energy (Chi) either through lifting, attracting, calming, deflecting, diverting, or stabilizing it. These are just some of the popular dance steps: use them as a beginning, then innovate, and use your creativity.

Reflective Surfaces and Mirrors are little bits of magic that probably seem a bit overused, but they're so helpful that for most people it's just too good a tool to resist. They do so many things. They make the room bigger, double things, flip them around, make things seem closer, move things to the other side of the room, bounce light all over the place. The list goes on and on. When you're using them, understand how they work. Think playfulness, think information, think light pressure. But remember, mirrors reflect other kinds of energy besides the visible wavelengths. Ultraviolet, electromagnetic, kinetic, sound, and all of their complex codes are also subject to the manipulating power of mirrors.

When faced with a long straight hallway where energy rushes, some light pressure from a mirror placed at the end is just what you need to slow it down. Reflective surfaces on the front of pictures work like mirrors to a great extent, so if you wish to slow energy down in that hallway, alternating pictures along the side walls creates sources of light pressure that cross the energy path and stagger its pace. They also work effectively to bounce light into that dark area.

For good conversation, make sure that there are a sufficient number of reflective surfaces in the room. They encourage the flow of energy back and forth between the speakers. When giving a presentation, place yourself in front of a reflective surface to maximize your message, and if you want to win a conversational point, maneuver your opponent so that they in turn have their back to a bare wall, or even better, a curtain or open doorway. The light pressure behind you reflects your words to them, but they have no inherent pressure helping them carry their ideas back toward you. A house isn't a home until you get the pictures up. There's nothing to carry your ideas around, so conversation lags. Real Estate agents hate to sell empty houses because it's so hard to get the prospective buyer to listen to their sales pitch. The sound-reflecting materials in museums puts you into whisper mode. Meeting rooms, whether they are for business or pleasure, need some pictures with reflective surfaces to spark conversation.

All forms of Light are powerful tools, this includes objects that illuminate, reflect or refract. Mirrors, electric lights, candles, cut crystals, and windows all become important elements in Feng Shui. Light is information. How do telephones send our words, faxes, and e-mails? With coded light inside fiber-optic cable! A 150 years ago this concept sounded like magic. Now we call it physics, and accept it readily. Light is also related to the dynamic side of Chi, Yang, where dark is related to the responsive side of Chi, Yin. Let's look at these polarities again. Light and shadow describe it well. Dynamic and responsive are closer to the mark, because they more fully describe the complexity of Chi. Positive and negative work fine as electrical terms, but not for living issues, and they are too clumsy a pair of definitions to use with complex moral or spiritual issues. Dynamic and responsive more closely describe the beautiful ebb and flow of life, of male and female, and the ever-unfolding, and delightful play that both love and loving engender, whether it be in the dark or the light.

Light plays the role of the dynamic, and it creates movement around it through its creation of heat and its ability to transmit and translate information. By washing away the shadows, light allows us to recognize our sources of energy and our centers of activity, and our areas of focus.

On the other hand, due to our over-dependence on electricity, artificial light is playing havoc with the human anatomy. When choosing light sources, for the sake of healthy eyes and lives, combine electrical and natural sources together. Natural light from windows and skylights can be maximized through the use of reflective glass on pictures, mirrors, and even polished floors. Add incandescent light sources where needed. Fluorescent and halogen lamps add new hazards to our environments. Endless banks of fluorescent bulbs in windowless offices are not only demoralizing, but they are dangerous for those with low thresholds to seizures and nervous disorders. The high-speed flicker short-circuits the human nervous system. Computer and television screens add the same disruptive component. None should be used without some natural or incandescent light sources, because their steady light helps overcome this problem. The electromagnetic field from the ballast in fluorescent fixtures and halogen gas add additional health concerns to our environment.

Music of all dimensions and harmonious sounds, bells, wind chimes, musical instruments, music boxes, the radio or stereo, your own lovely voice, are all powerful tools for adjusting energy flows. If you want to change the vibration of any space, just break into song!

Having a dominant chime that you love the sound of on the front door helps all the other tones created by energy flowing through the space to sound more clearly. The tones in the room become less haphazard and more ordered. This helps create harmony in the home, because if everyone knows their place and responsibilities within the family, or office, everything goes more smoothly.

So keep this thought in mind anytime you use a musical instrument; When you create music, you are translating between the solid and nonsolid worlds, and the patterns you impress with these energy tools accumulate in the environment and affect them for the better. Chimes and bells are a wonderful influence if your space is the scene of arguments, incessantly ringing phones, and disruptive noise, because the sweet song of the chimes works at overriding the discordance with harmony. They repaint the area with beauty and signify the sounds of home. They can provide the extra electrons, the environmental antioxidants necessary to repair the free radicals from pollution hanging onto your coattails as you walk through the door. Their sound pressure can push away the outer world and tell your body that you are home again, and safe.

That small chime that we hang on our hotel room door, from the doorstop or knob, turns it into our home for a while, and makes our bodies feel safer when we sleep. The sound seems to please the staff, since they are unfailingly courteous and considerate when we do this, filled with smiles when they see us, and taking special care with our rooms. After all, who doesn't love beautiful music?

The Living Spark and the Water that nurtures it are tools, but what's a living thing? Does it breathe? That may be one definition. Of course, we've known stones that would qualify as alive, so don't be so quick to write lists that exclude  anything. Generally plants, cut flowers, herbs, aquariums, fountains, birdbaths, and animals add a little spark into a stagnant environment. After all, one interpretation of Chi is breath, so that breath, whether it's oxygen or carbon dioxide, can generally be depended upon to introduce some Chi into the room! Remember that plants both clean the air of the room and they contribute to the amount of oxygen that we enjoy there.

Moving Objects move energy and are essential if you want to keep your life moving! The only constant is change, correct? Well maybe! But either way things like mobiles, banners, flags, whirligigs, plants, windmills, thrive on the breath of change, and actively contribute to it. What we want to avoid in Feng Shui and life is stagnation. So tools that dance in the face of change are great for overcoming that low energy vortex that forms underneath the clutter. Remember that anything that moves receives energy and translates it into another form. This creates an environment ripe for change. A good trick for construction sites where work is stalled is to hang a couple of mobiles or crystals in the stagnant areas. This technique seems to pull the contractors back pretty quickly, so when they reappear on the scene, make sure you're ready to grab them and put them to work.

Stabilizing Objects. Sometimes we don't want things to change quite so much. Or we need to create an earthy focus to bring a runaway situation back down to the ground. Sometimes people who are lacking any Earth signs (Taurus, Virgo, or Capricorn) in their natal charts need something like this to balance their natural flightiness. Heavy stones and statues, symbolic sculptures, natural crystals, seashells, and rocks all serve as anchors. Suppose you travel too much for work and want more time at home. The judicious placement of an anchor in the Section Nine (travel) and

Section Four (home) will keep the suitcases locked in the attic.

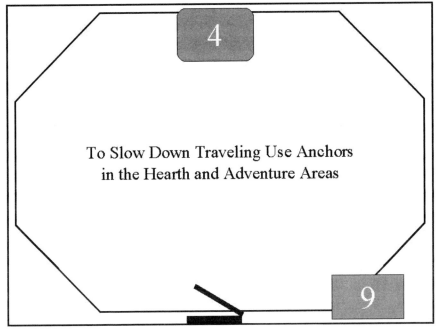

To Slow Down Traveling Use Anchors
in the Hearth and Adventure Areas

Another application might be for a child who needs a bit of grounding to accomplish more at school. Stabilizing Sections 3, 6 and 11 will help focus their attention on the work at hand. Of course it wouldn't hurt to take that TV out of their child's bedroom!

So What's the Influence of Electricity?
Keeping in mind how recent an addition this is to our environments, don't make any quick assumptions about the good and bad aspects of electromagnetics in our lives. Also, the "traditional rules of Feng Shui" never figured on Morse, Edison, and Marconi, so when it comes to electronics, computers, fans, lights, appliances and their ilk, you just have to use your brain and your instincts. While it's good to light up the stagnant areas of your space, for instance, a stereo in the resource or nurturing areas can activate those

aspects of your life, respect the body's programming. We need a break from electrical stimulation, especially while relaxing or sleeping. Keep yourself at more than arm's length from clock radios, TVs, stereos, and computers. The best thing to do is to throw the microwave out the window along with the clock radio. This is good advice for any flesh-and-blood creature, whether that creature is covered with skin, fur, scales, or feathers. If you find that your life is hopelessly disorganized and your nervous system is overtaxed, then you might want to make it a habit to protect yourself from electronic pollution from electrical sources. They disrupt the electromagnetic field of the body and drain the body of minerals, most notably magnesium, the relaxation mineral. Electrical fields make the body tense, and then the body must draw upon the magnesium reserves in the muscles to make the blood vessels relax. If you're around electrical fields enough you'll run out of your magnesium reserves, this can result in muscle tension, constipation, anxiety, and heart attacks. Those are a few of the not-so-pleasant results.

Also very important to note is that not everyone reacts to electricity equally. Some folks are much more sensitive, and that sensitivity can vary over the course of their lives. For instance, during the ages of thirty-nine and forty-one, (sometimes called "mid-life crisis time for men, and "redefinition" for women) a person can become much more sensitive due to the body's electromagnetic field becoming overcharged by planetary transits. When a planet travels through a section of the sky that is angular (or very tension producing) in relation to the position it, or another important planet, held at a person's birth, that person can develop certain sensitivities. That mid life crisis period is a hot spot for electromagnetic sensitivity. Your change in energy attracts ambient energy. If you are having trouble sleeping, be especially aware of artificial light sources filtering into the sleeping area. The human body is designed to fall asleep in gradually deepening darkness. The hormonal system is keyed to this, and excessive, constant light sources in the bedroom cause all kinds of problems. What starts with sleep problems often leads to a loss of sex drive. A recent survey showed that 40 percent of relationships break up due to sleep deprivation, and another claimed that fully 70 percent of Americans have sleep disorders. If you're having a problem sleeping the first step is tossing that clock radio and replacing it with a battery operated clock, which you can find at any travel store. Its direct current batteries won't be read as light by the pineal gland. The alternating current of a clock radio is too much like lightening for the body to relax around it. The eyes register light through the closed eyelids. At 4:00 AM, if the room is not sufficiently dark, the pineal gland won't reset properly. This gland is the body's timekeeper: It synchronizes the functions of the pituitary, thyroid, thymus, pancreas, adrenals, and reproductive organs. If the pineal gland is not clear about what time it is (the darkest part of the night), then this cascade of hormonal reactions doesn't happen in its proper sequence, the body's timing is thrown off and all kinds of problems arise. It's like trying to dance the Tango with no sense of rhythm, or your ears plugged up: It makes it hard to look good on the dance floor, even if you have a great partner.

The Power of Symbolic Objects! When you look at a beautiful picture and your spirit experiences that intake of breath known as inspiration, you don't usually consider that in one sense, that picture is just a piece of paper or canvas with ink or paint on it. What we focus on is an equally valid reality, the power of the image to influence, guide, and communicate with us. A photo is a symbol, as is a painting or sculpture. Be aware of how they affect you. Symbolic languages have power over us because they speak through the shapes of the body, and the natural world around us: This language was impressed upon us in our earliest physiological programming. The use of traditional, symbolic objects is most effective if you have a positive relationship to them. If you hate the way the solutions look, not only will it reduce their effectiveness, but your emotional responses to them may also cause other problems in your life.

Of course, an original piece of art infused with the artist's energy is no small thing. Why does a famous painting like DaVinci's Mona Lisa have such power? Because overlaying the canvas and paint is the energy of a genius, together with all of the visual Chi of every person who has viewed it through the centuries. We arrive before the Mona Lisa with the thought in our minds that this is a famous and wonderful piece of art. This is high cultural drama! It explains a bit about why museums are such great places to dance the Tango.

Images are most useful where people will see them often. That's where the picture's or objects get charged up by our positive feelings! Your mind believes what it sees. It's very easy to program the thinking process with images. We can't say too many times "Make sure that every room has a powerful, and uplifting focus, to catch your attention as soon as you walk through the door". It makes the mind focus, and this makes the body operate more smoothly, and this is what keeps a room neat and focused. During consultations, wives will say that they can't convince their husbands to take a vacation. We'll suggest that they put some photos of where they would like to go on the refrigerator, a place pretty much everybody in the house frequents, looking for satisfaction, and getting it. Soon that image and pleasure are related in everyone's mind. Next thing you know, it's the husband who's saying, "We need to go someplace warm, with a beach and no telephones." So the wife says "Good idea Honey." And pushes the speed dial button on the phone for the travel agency. It's like magic! Men being more easily visually stimulated, are easier to program with images. This is something that most wives know, and there's nothing wrong with that. We're sure that a wife's right to manage her husband for his own good and the good of the family, is firmly tucked away into our unspoken marriage vows. The I Ching is quite clear about the reality that the happiness of the family is dependent upon the intelligence and constancy of the wife. Anyone who sells houses or furniture will tell you that it's the wife who decides what the family is going to buy. While men are easier to program with visual clues, women are easier to program through the sense of smell. All flowers may be beautiful, but the scent of the rose reaches out and touches the heart.

There are Many Theories Related to the Use of Color, and in fact we have an entire chapter devoted to color based upon our experience. One thing that you need to know up front is that not everything related to color translates cross-culturally, so don't be too quick with the hard-and-fast traditional rules. Some of our reactions to color are based upon societal programming. For instance, in the United States, the combination of red, white, and blue found in the American flag has powerful and not so subtle emotional connotations that were programmed in us, from early childhood. So use colors wisely, whether in the form of plants, flowers, tapestries, paintings, posters, upholstery, window treatments, wall coverings, carpets, doors, or whatever. The one universal rule is that color has a profound influence, so be conscious of it. Red is used often in Feng Shui because it is an energizer, but if you absolutely hate red, it can't possibly create happy Chi in your environment. Your human energy is the primary source of Chi in your home. Use colors that are pleasing to you and that make you happy. Sad colors make for sad Chi, and happy colors make happy Chi. See! It's not that complicated: The Tango seems much more difficult. Designers love monochromatics and muted tones, but these often result in unfocused, cluttered environments. Remember: Color is a primary tool in Feng Shui, and by omitting strong colors you invite chaos.

Be the Creative Spark! In other words, rely on your feelings and instincts. Make it up as you go along, creating solutions that fit the space and its unique nature. Design is a creative field, and Feng Shui seeks creative solutions. Feng Shui is neither predominantly right-brained nor left-brained, but the best practitioners are those that have a good analytical and technical basis in terms of the workings of the human body, the sciences, and engineering of buildings, and then tap freely into their subconscious and intuitive talents. It's like dancing. First you learn the pattern of steps, then you to listen to the music and tap your foot until it's moving around inside you. Then you firmly, but gently wrap your arms around your partner, and then, let your passion be your guide.

Chapter Seven
A Universal Checklist
The Things Everyone Needs to Know

In the course of doing lots of workshops we found that a good format was to have two evenings of lecture, followed by an evening of mini-consultations done for the group using individual floor plans provided by each person. After a while we found it wise to ask everyone to save any questions for the final part of the lecture. The simple fact was that we were (more than likely) going to answer their questions in the course of the lecture. Why? Because people tend to have the same kinds of problems! Life has some standard, or universal, challenges we all have to learn to deal with. These are the types of things people ask questions about. Also many people fall victim to the same Feng Shui faux pas because they live in similar, poorly designed buildings.

Much of the depersonalization and dissatisfaction that people are suffering from in their homes and work environments is due to architectural trends from the past several decades. The result is that we keep seeing the same kinds of problems popping up again and again and again. After awhile, you'd think that you could do this work with a simple checklist. For some basic stuff, that's true.

Carry around this list and you would have "Do-It-Yourself Feng Shui". Just follow the checklist and find happiness. It's amazing how often fixing the simple ergonomic and energetic lapses can improve an environment's ability to help people be happy. Of course, there's the subtle shifting and mingling of human energetic emotions, planetary lines, energetic pathways, and their ability to enhance lives (or play havoc with them) that really keeps practitioners on their toes. A professional who works with this all the time will easily see things that other people never notice, but there's a tremendous amount that people can and should do for themselves. We have touched upon some of the concepts already, but bear with the repetition of these crucial points as we explore them in greater depth.

Issue One. The Importance the Front Door. Failing to use the front door is a problem created by the automobile society and the ever-increasing movement in building practices that seems to want to prevent people from ever going outside. You work inside all day. Then leave from a subterranean garage. From there you go through the drive-in bank to get money, then perhaps, stop at the drive-through dry cleaners to pick up your business suits. Then you go through the drive-through pizzeria to pick up your dinner (which you ordered in advance on your cell phone). You arrive home by driving into the garage, which you opened with your automatic garage-door opener. Scary! Aside from the issues of over insulation from nature and forgetting what color the sky is, a Feng Shui faux pas arises because the front door is the representative of the social position in the society. That's being completely ignored!

One question which we answer often during workshops, which would have been unheard of 100 years ago is, "Which is the front door?" To orient the Bagua, we select the door that obviously was designed to fulfill that position and is identified as such by passers-by. Many people in the suburbs never use that front door. It can be worse yet if the front door is not obvious, hidden behind overgrown bushes, or if there are multiple doors on the front of the house. These issues give us our first clue as to why the client hasn't gotten any promotions or raises in quite a while, and why their kids are unclear about their future career paths. The pathway to achievement is obscured.

Think of the front door as the place where your flag sails above your castle. The banner says, "This is what I do, and this is the role I fulfill in society". This role may the same route by which you earn your money, although it may be different, because reputation (or notoriety) and earnings are two diverse functions. For example, we always think of the Venetian, Titian, as a great painter of portraits, but he made more money from selling lumber than from painting. Goethe is known to the world as a great poet, yet he made his living as a botanist. See the difference? In Western Society, it's not unusual for a person's social position to be identical to their method of earning a living, but they are not always synonymous. As we mentioned before reputation and income are represented by two different sections of the Bagua. In fact the earning of money relates to a number of spots on the Bagua working interactively, sections 3, 6, and 1, to just name a few.

What happens if a family ignores that front door? Their social position stagnates. They have problems at work from a lack of acknowledgment. We did a consultation for four women who shared a house. All had good professional positions, but they were all suffering from problems centered on their coworkers and partners not giving them credit for their efforts. Lack of recognition. The house was designed so that the front door was more symbolic than usable. The garage entrance and the back door led immediately into the family room and served as their main entrance. But to the world driving by, that big, formal front door that they never used was their front door. The front door was their recognition, and the women were not accessing that energy. The Universe likes obvious signs. We knew there was a problem when we went to open the door from the inside. First, we had to move a carpet out of the way. Then we had to tug open the stuck and squeaky door. Then we stepped outside into a puddle of water on the steps. The two ornate coach lamps were not only burned out, but they were also broken. So here we saw stagnation, frustrated energy, and lack of access. All of the things they were experiencing in their careers. It doesn't take a rocket scientist to figure this one out, folks!

So did they take our advice? Yes and no. One of the owners moved her office into a room at the front of the house, adjacent to the front door. That shifted energy to sections of the Bagua that relate to career. They straightened up the front door, but they also came to a realization that acclaim was not an important part of their plan, so they didn't change their traffic patterns. Making a home and personal development was more important to them. The two younger women for whom career was more important moved out and the older women settled into an energetic design that more suited their needs.

One of the basic requirements on our checklist is that every door to the outside world have a sweet sounding chime on it. The placement is especially nice because the chimes resonate even when they are seemingly standing still. Whenever any one enters the house or workspace they hear the song of the chimes, and the song lifts their energy. Together human and chime paint a pleasant color all around the entranceway. After a while, everyone who comes in that door starts to feel better. Use different chimes on each exterior door so you'll know which one is being opened. The front door chime needs to be the dominant one, just as the parents need to be the dominant force in the house. This is especially helpful if you have young children at home. The chimes on the doors are symbolic of the parents' voices. Hearing that chime as they come in the door puts thoughts of the parent back in their heads. So when kids come in with muddy feet they hear the chime, and they know that Mom or Dad are going to know who left that trail up the stairs. The kids stop and wipe their feet. Like magic, right?

Always make sure the front door looks good, creates a good first impression, and works well, with no squeaky hinges. It should be well lit (consider putting the lights on a timer if you don't use the door often) and be easily accessible. In that way, you'll ensure that your career will have the same qualities.

Can people easily determine which door is your front door? The last thing you want is confusion about your face to the world. If it's not clear, make it clear! Paint the front door a bright color. The color you choose should pleasantly contrast with the face of the house. Place the mailbox beside it. Put a wreath on it, and perhaps the family name. Then obscure the secondary doors by painting them the same color as the rest of the house and plant some bushes around them so they fade into the scenery. Apartment dwellers take note! If you want to be noticed in your career, make your door noticeable.

Issue Two. A Happy Bed. What is more representative of a relationship than the bed? We are constantly amazed when people tell us that they just can't seem to get a relationship going, and then we see that the bed is pushed up against the wall! Is the person really open to a relationship? No! Another person would literally have to climb over them, or worse, ask permission to get in and out of bed. Placing the bed with its side against the wall cramps the aura and throws it out of shape, often affecting the person's self-image. This prevents them from being open to relationships.

Depending upon which side of the bed is against the wall causes slightly different problems. Normally your body will turn onto its back at about 4:00 AM to allow the

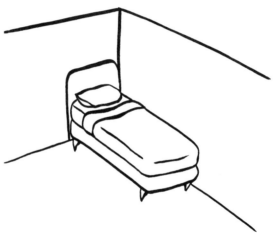

A Bed that Crunches the Left Side of the Aura Hurts the Self Image

lungs to properly ventilate and recharge themselves. This coincides with the time at which the aura is recharged, so we're talking about which side of the body is next to the wall when lying flat on your back. If the left side of the body is against the wall, the sense of self-worth is compressed and dulled. So while those people may be open to relationships, their suppressed self-image might attract people of a lower vibration than their own, someone who is less than their ideal mate. If the right side of the body (the partnership side) is compressed, then the ability to relate with others is dulled. A rule of thumb is never sleep close enough to a wall that you can touch it with your outstretched hand, unless you want to screw up

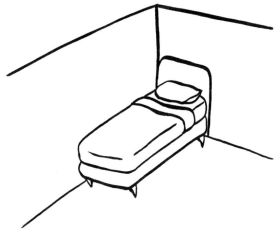

A Bed that Crunches the Right Side of the Aura Hurts the Ability to Reach Out to Others

your relationships and self-image, of course. This is, after all, a free-will Universe.

Parents, take note. This is a classic mistake made with children's beds. What kinds of problems do children have in school? They either suffer from low self-esteem or have difficulty getting along with their peers. Even infants do better with their sides free. The auras of children are flexible, so keep their heads close to the wall, to anchor their crown chakra and allow them to feel secure. This even helps babies sleep through the night. Just keep their heads away from the electrical sockets unless you want them to have frizzy hair and a fuzzy head.

Couples need equal access to the relationship/bed. The paths on either side should be fairly equal. Single people need to provide this access for a partner if they want their energy to attract another person into their life. If you wish to increase communication between a couple there should be reflective surfaces on both sides of the bed, either mirrors or reflective glass over pictures. These reflect the couple's auras back and forth to each other as they sleep, and this helps communication. Make sure they can't see themselves in any reflective surface when they are lying down. The body can be pulled out of a deep sleep because the eye registers your own reflected

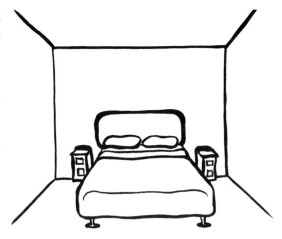

The Bed Centered in the Bedroom Helps the Aura Maintain Balance

movement, or that of the spouse or pet, through the closed eyelids. Some practitioners feel there should not be any mirrors in the bedroom. The secret to using them effectively has to do with the height at which they are placed on the wall. They should not be placed too low. The guideline is that you should not be able to see your torso reflected in the glass when you are sitting up in the bed. The taller person

using the bed should be able to see nothing lower than their head. The problem this placement avoids is over excitement of the emotional aura during sleep. The benefit is that the more stable parts of the auras are mixed together. When you reflect this area of the aura back and forth between a

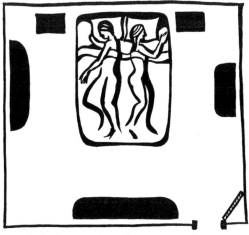

A Balanced Bedroom Makes a Balanced Life

couple, they begin to intuitively know what the other wants and needs. This is generally a good thing for the longevity of the relationship.

Issue Three. Sleeping Free from Environmental Stress. Sleeping under a beam or at the point of an angle can create serious health problems by exposing the person to subtle but cumulative stress from the pressure of the angle. When the weight of a building is being carried on a beam, or transferred to a vertical structural member, the weight has to be passed on. To where? Well, remember gravity. Earth energy flows towards the center of the Earth. If there is an exposed structural beam above the person's body, where does the pressure of its weight go? It travels through the person! Now, don't worry, there's ways to fix that without ripping the house apart. And if the beam is inside drywall or the plaster of a ceiling, it's not a problem, because the compressive energy is distributed out through the surfaces. What we're talking about here are those picturesque and trendy open-beam ceilings that photograph so well for design magazines.

We solve the problem by diverting the force. The traditional use of flutes placed at the juncture of the beam and wall served as a type of grounding tool. Energy doesn't flow smoothly around a sharp corner: So you need to create a bend, a path of least resistance, so the pressure transfers from the beam to the walls smoothly. While the flutes work well, in Western interiors we prefer ornamental corner brackets.

When they are placed at the intersection of beam and wall, they serve as a kind of energetic rainspout. Otherwise the flow gets congested and blocked at the juncture, somewhat like a traffic jam at a busy intersection. Then the pressure starts backing up until it pours down within the archway or room, creating a wall of pressure that will adversely affect anyone spending much time underneath it.

A spot solution is to hang a refracting crystal in the shape of a globe from the beam under which the person is sitting or sleeping. As light and other types of energy are refracted through the crystal, due to its configuration, a crystal will create a curved energetic flow shaped like an umbrella around itself. Pressure coming off the beams will be caught in this dome-shaped current and carried off to the side. The span of the beam that this creates an umbrella for is dependent upon the size of the refracting globe. A crystal won't fix a whole room, but it can make a chair or bed more comfortable and healthy to use.

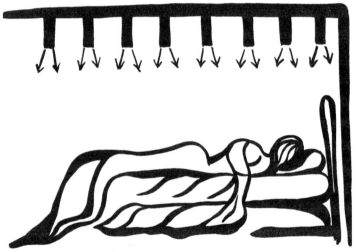

*The Body is Powerfully
Stressed by Beams During Sleep*

This situation is even more difficult when the beams are a different color than the ceiling above, so the person lying down is seeing a series of lines. The most basic programs in the body's autonomic nervous system read straight lines as claws. If these beams are down low, close to the body, such as a sloping ceiling coming down towards the head of a bed, the effect is intensified.

We did a consultation where the rooms of the two daughters, who were away at college, both had low-beamed ceilings that angled above the beds. Both rooms were complete disasters. The only clear spots were little sections on the beds just big enough to sleep on. These girls literally did nothing but sleep in the rooms. The tension levels were so bad that they were much happier away at school. Of course, this probably was not intentional, but it fits in with our basic axiom: "Don't make your guest room too comfortable." Next time you see the movie Sleepless in Seattle, check out Tom Hanks' bedroom in Seattle. Low beams pointed down at his head. No wonder he couldn't sleep. Where did he sleep instead? On the couch, with his left side against the cushions. Something which tends to hurt the self-image, and boy, was he depressed! The house sat on the bay, where the water reinforced his emotionality. He didn't need to put his son on the radio to find a girlfriend. He just needed to find a different bedroom.

Placing the bed where the person trying to sleep in it can't command the door makes that person feel vulnerable and unable to relax completely. Why? Because the animal body will not relax unless it can defend itself with a fair chance of success. For any of you who have cats, do you ever walk into a room and see your cat's butt pointing at you? It's always their face you see first. Ms. Kitty will not completely relax for her 20 hours of daily beauty sleep unless she can know with the faintest lifting of a lazy eyelid, "Am I going to be stroked, or do I have to run?" Humans deal with this same dilemma, but they tend to ignore it. Why? Because the conscious mind knows that the dogs are here at home, the alarm is on, and you are generally safe. But the body doesn't care! The body's design is much older than the logical mind, and its criteria are much simpler. If your body can't command the entrance to the room from a distance that offers some chance for a ready response in the case of danger, and at an angle that offers sufficient perspective so that your body can tell how quickly the adversary is moving, you won't completely relax.

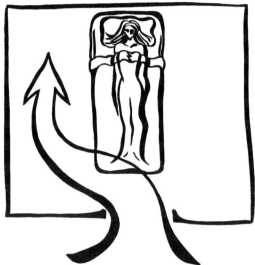

Having Your Feet Facing the Door is a Prescription for Foot Pain

Of course, the obvious solution is to move the bed. But sometimes that's not possible, placing a mirror so that the person can see the door is helpful. Why are we doing that? Simple, we're tricking the body into believing the door is on the other side of the room, where it can command it. The body will tend to believe what it sees. This is not as good a solution as moving the bed, but it's a good second choice. If the pathway of energy coming in the door is causing disruptive problems, it might be wise to place a friendly piece of crystal like rose quartz on the bed stand as a buffer to protect your energy. The body is thousands of times more sensitive to all kinds of energy when sleeping than when it is awake. Whenever a person sleeps directly in the pathway from the door, it will cause them problems. We were doing a consultation where the energy flowed into the room and immediately caught the husband in the shoulder and lower neck. Lahni said: "Well I don't know who is sleeping here, but they're waking up with neck and shoulder pains every morning." The husband said: "It's true, I do. How did you know that?" With a wave of the hand, she said: "I'm magic". Then she breezed out of the room, leaving Ralph to explain the dynamics at work.

Remember, when energy flows into the room in the Northern Hemisphere it will tend to go to the left and work its way around the room in a clockwise direction.

Energy Moves Clockwise in the North

If the sleeping person is directly in that path, they're going to be plugged into this current and under a great deal of strain nightly.

Shoes under the bed are a prescription for nightmares. So unless you want those "Mares" leaving hoof prints all over your bedroom, get those shoes out of there. When you're standing

Sleeping Directly in the Energy Pathway Creates Stress and Pain. Don't Do It!

up at your job, or in a store, or shopping, what part of you

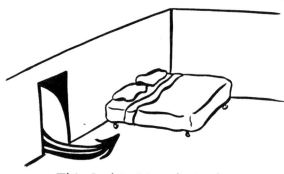

This Bed is Directly in the Curving Energy Pathway

is actually in contact with the physical world? The soles of your shoes! They pick up vibrations that are both good and bad. So if you work, shop, or walk in very stressful environments, the soles of your shoes are drenched in negative vibrations. Then you wear them home, toss them under your bed, and wonder why you can't get away from your job. We'll come in and you say: "Even at night I'll lay in bed and think about my work." Then we lift the skirt of the bed and see your shoes under there, oozing their troubling vibrations into your dreams. Protect your sleepy haven: Without it everything else in life falls apart.

A word of advice. To cleanse the soles of your shoes, walk over a lawn, beach, or wooded path, because the Earth will absorb and transmute those energies. In any case let those puppies cool at

Who's Hiding Under there?

the front door for a couple of days, then carry them (don't wear them) into the bedroom if you must, and lock them up in the closet. We've had more clients with chronic nightmares be freed from those nasty "equine" visitations simply by getting all of the shoes out of their bedroom.

Think of the energy flowing into a room as a stream. It flows past the bed, and your emotional body drinks from it. Well, the last thing you want to do is pollute that stream with the disruptive vibrations from the outer world that you definitely don't want to invite into your inner sanctum. Another way to envision it is to realize that, as you sleep, your electromagnetic field expands. If you sleep too close to the door, then you have a lot of electrical current running past your bed. When you lie down, your field plugs into this current. If the current is carrying a lot of static, then it's picked up in your aura, and that results in head and neck aches. If it's pointed at your feet you may start having foot and ankle problems.

Issue Four. Comfortable Chairs. Placing chairs so their backs are to a door? What were you thinking? This is a double-edged sword that adversely affects both those people sitting in the chairs and those entering the room.

If this is at a desk or worktable, the space will usually be a mess. Because the person with their back to the door has their flight or flight reflex turned on. The tension emanating from their body will saturate the space until they don't want to stay there one minute longer than absolutely necessary to get the job (or the meal) done. From the other point of view, for the person entering, to immediately encounter the back of a chair is very emotionally and physically weakening. It's like having someone turn their back on you during a conversation.

If a sales office is set up with the chair backs facing the door, the deal is sabotaged as soon as the prospect walks into the room. People don't commit to serious investments if they feel weak. Just angle those chairs around so their fronts are at least three-quarters towards the door and they look inviting. Then clients will feel strong enough to sign on the dotted line. This concept of commanding the door is primary to successful design. It has a major effect on how we feel in a space, on our every thought, and our approach to every project we tackle. The body wants to command the door.

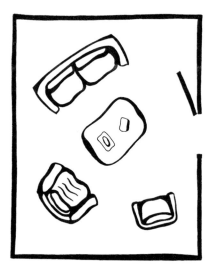

These Chairs Welcome You into the Room

The next time you walk through a large office complex, check out the desk placements of the various managers and employees. Invariably the movers and shakers of the company will have a good command of the door, even to the point where they may directly face it. They are programming their minds and body that whatever comes through their door, they are ready for it. In fact, they invite new experiences.

Among administrators who work in a cooperative manner the most typical desk placement is sideways to the door. This is akin to sitting next to a teammate on the bench, ready to elicit another person's opinions,

Sitting Sideways to Door Forces Cooperation

and a willingness to sublimate one's own ideas for the needs of the group.

When the positioning of the desk is three-quarters to the door, then we have a combination of both programs running. The person is willing to cooperate, but still intends to have a commanding position in the partnership. This is a position that we find among the financial officers, or possibly a company founder who has a talent for finding creative and dynamic staff. They appreciate their staff's get-up-and-go but they know that they themselves have a lot to contribute.

Facing Three Quarters to the Door Shares Power Well

When a person voluntarily places themselves in a vulnerable position, in other words, with their back to the door, in a pathway, or under a tall cabinet, we find they usually had a domineering parent. During their formative years someone (literally or figuratively) was always looking over their shoulder and putting pressure on them. They've become so accustomed to this level of tension that they consider it normal, and they expect it when they're working. The person uses this tension producing chair placement to put pressure on them, that same familiar pressure they grew up with. Some people may not be able to work effectively, except in that type of situation.

Sometimes we see situations where a person will have two work tables, one facing the door, and the other with its back to the door. When the person needs to get something important done, they'll face away from the door. This especially works for those who are visually oversensitive. By turning their back to the door they cut out the visual distraction of people passing in the hall.

A great deal of Feng Shui consulting is about reducing unnecessary stress. However, there is such a thing as necessary stress: The pressure that needs to be applied to accomplish a task. That type of stress is better applied in small doses. There are times when you realize that it's not broken, so don't fix it. The sign that it's working for the person, is that the desk is facing away from the door, but it's neat. In those cases don't go changing it. But when it's a chronic, and problematic state, that type of stress needs to be addressed

If the desk looks like a bomb hit it, it's not working for the person, and we need to talk. Just remember, even if you're one of those high pressure individuals that need a high pressure desk, nothing says you can't have a rear-view-mirror, to boost your efficiency, and save your neck muscles.

A more common occurrence is where the person is working with their back to the door, through little choice of their own. This either happens through placing a desk in a small room, where the person has sought to maximize the open floor space, or the person has been assigned a desk in a cubicle arrangement within an office complex.

The cubicle arrangement is very popular in large corporate and government offices, and they are almost

The Cubicle Trap

always designed where the only place to sit is with the back to the door. As a result, the dynamic that is set up is the predator/prey reflex. In other words, when we walk up behind a sitting person, we are descending upon them from above, very much in the way that a feline would pounce on the back of the neck of their prey. The person in the chair is the prey. So every interaction that the person has with anyone entering their cubicle starts off with this feeling of weakness and vulnerability.

Again, the solution here is to move the desk if possible, or place a mirror in a position where the occupant can command the door. Not only do you want the person at the desk to be able to see the person

Cubicle Tigers can be Hungry and Bold

entering the space, but you also want the first thing anyone entering the office to see is the eyes of the office's occupant. This is very much like coming upon a wild animal's reflective eyes in the night with a flashlight. As soon as you see the eyes, you freeze in place. That's the kind of challenge you need to create when you are sitting with your back to the door.

Placing a rear-view mirror on the edge of the computer screen is a simple solution.

If you doubt the importance of a simple mirror, then remember back to a time when you lost your rear-view-mirror in your car. Your body keeps looking for the mirror even though your mind knows it's not there, and every time you do look, there's a shock of insecurity.

Solutions Don't Have to Cost a Lot

Why? Because when we're driving, we're making life and death decisions based on a little piece of reflective glass. But to our body and our emotional nature, it makes all the difference. If the boss asks why there's a mirror on your computer, just explain that it's more efficient. When people come in, you don't have to stop typing, taking your fingers off the keys, twisting your spine, and interrupting the thought traveling along it from your mind to your fingers. All this just to see that it's the mail boy coming in, or someone taking a wrong turn. Next thing you know the boss will be asking where they can buy mirrors for the other offices.

Another dynamic that is at work is the sensitivity of your spine. Remember that the spinal cord is the main electrical conduit connecting your brain to your body, and it is very sensitive to external fields. This is one of the reasons that a seat in a restaurant with its back to a busy walkway is so annoying. The spine, and especially the neck, want to be protected. So when you're sitting at an office desk, with your back to the door, it can be a good idea to place a piece of fabric on the back of the chair. This offers your back some additional protection. If the cloth is strongly colored, and has a positive connotation for you, it's especially effective. However, you should not use anything in the red range, since that triggers the predator reflex. Light Pink, yellow, tan, lavender, or purple all work well. In situations that are especially adversarial, we have suggested (albeit tongue in cheek) that they place a tiger skin

Command the Tiger and She Becomes a Pussy Cat

print on the back of the chair. That predator print, plus your eyes in the mirror really puts the "intruder" on notice in a very subtle way.

Issue Five. A Healthy Stove. Placing the stove so the cook has their back to the main kitchen door is a surefire recipe for stress. The location of the stove is one of the three most important places in the house from a traditional Feng Shui perspective (together with the front door and the bed). After all, the stove is the source of all nourishment. If the cook is feeling vulnerable and tense the entire time they're cooking, when they bring the meal to the table they might as well ask "How would you like your tension tonight?"

The only good thing about an arrangement where the cook cannot command the door is that when they go to sell the house, the stove will probably look great, simply because it was used so little. We've seen many cases where the stove was badly placed, but the occupants had purchased a microwave that they put on a counter, which allowed them to command the door (additionally the reflective faces of most microwaves overcomes this problem), and they did all their cooking using the microwave.

Of course, it's best to position the stove so that the cook is in complete command of the door. It's helpful to remember that when we're cooking, we're working with hot pots, pans, liquids and foods. It's very easy to get burned or scalded. There's steam, and sometimes smoke, and definitely aromas from the meal in process, so the situation is highly reactive. This may give us a better idea of how a person's electromagnetic field can imbue the food with their energy. So we want to make sure that the energy is as positive and healthy as possible. We don't want feelings of vulnerability and fear becoming infused in that food along with the flavors. This is a powerful enough factor that we've had clients rip out wall-mounted stoves, place them in islands in the center of the kitchen, and then rave about the results. This is a practical and healthy solution and a lot easier if it's built correctly in the first place. Stoves are placed along the walls, not for the convenience of the cooks, but for the ease of the builders. But remember who is paying for the

Island Stoves Allow You to Command Your Domain

house, and who is going to live in it.

You may be in a position where that option is not possible. For instance, you may be renting, or in possession of a spouse with a less-than-understanding disposition. Then you might want to place a mirror, a reflective picture, a reflective back splash, mirror tiles, or a convection oven with a reflective door above the stove. This allows the cook to relax and command the door. Remember that rear-view-mirror. The body just needs a clue in order to relax, but it really likes that clue.

Issue Six. Providing a Focus for the Eye. We've mentioned this several times but it's important enough that we're going to explore it again, adding in a couple of extra dimensions. This is the major problem of failing to provide a definite focus for the eye and other senses to fix upon when you go through that cave mouth, or enter a room. Why do they call it a cave 'mouth'? Because we know that something in there might eat us. This is special sin of the current school of neutral decorating, where everything is a variation of the same color and shade. Without a clear focus in each room, your life becomes unfocused.

Here is the dynamic at work. When you walk into a new space (never mind that you've been in the room a hundred times, to your body there is only right now) if your eyes scan back and forth and stay in motion, the fight-or-flight reflex is turned on. Why? Because as far as our body is concerned, we are emerging from the woods and crossing a meadow, and our eyes are scanning the fields of grasses, watching out for that saber-toothed tiger.

Let's repeat that exercise from Chapter Two. Move your head back and forth for about 10 seconds without letting your eyes settle on a single thing. Notice where the energy moves to in your body! The tension will be in your upper chest. That's fight-or-flight. The body is getting ready to take a breath and run if necessary, either from or after something. In fight-or-flight, we are ready to be prey or predator. We don't know which until we see what's making that movement in the grass. One thing we do know is that this is not the tension that we want to be painting on the entranceways to our rooms.

There's actually a psychological technique based upon this forced eye motion. It was found that, if a person recalled traumatic scenes while rapidly moving the eyes back and forth and not allowing them to focus on anything, the stressful memories lost much of their emotional impact.

Why does this work? Well, keep in mind that in a more natural world the body is designed to react to life-threatening and painful situations, either through giving battle or running away helter-skelter. In either case, while the person is experiencing the pain and  danger, their head and eyes are probably in constant motion from their legs pumping or their arms flailing.

The body's electrical system is designed in such a way that, during fight-or-flight any images received are restricted to the most exterior parts of the nervous system, where they can't get tied into the daily emotions. For it to be otherwise would cripple the person's ability to go out and gather food. They would be too fearful after a run-in with a predator. This method has proven most helpful for defusing the power of images that get locked into the brain. Routing the memories through a simulated fight-or-flight visual environment seems to erase the deeper connections, leaving only the surface reactions that are more manageable, being less profound.

So what's the result of not having a clear focus for your eyes when you enter a room? You can never seem to stay organized or finish anything! If it's simply unattractive clutter, then it simply propagates and dissolves into confusion. We had a client who lived in a three-room trailer. There wasn't a single focus for her eyes anywhere! When she entered, all she saw was piles of possessions, so she'd head to the next room to see the same thing, then retreat to the bedroom, which also lacked a focus, and end up in bed with the covers over her head.

In choosing a focus, it could be almost anything in terms of pictures, plants, or objects, just as long as it makes you feel good. Don't keep a pile of bills in their envelopes right by your front door. Make sure the first thing you see raises your energy, maybe even encourages that breath of delight that we experience when greeted with beauty. That's where the word aesthetic comes from: That intake of breath.

With another client, the first thing they saw was a huge basket filled with shoes of every kind and a long coat rack filled with an array of outer garments. If the first thing you see when you walk in your house are what you use to go back out again, the first thing your mind thinks of is going out again, and that's what you'll be doing, coming and going all the time. The same thing happens if you see a window or glass door to the outside as soon as you walk in. The mind is very easily programmed. In the first case, get those coats in the closet and get the excess shoes tucked away. In the second case, either put curtains up or hang something bright on the window (stained glass is nice) that keeps the focus of the eye inside rather than out. Remember, the body goes where the eyes are pointed, and what you look at first when you walk into a room is the recipient of a great deal of your primal, visual charge, and it in turn greatly affects you.

Another entrance difficulty is the popularity of homes with a center entrance foyer. The front door opens to a staircase, which immediately guides the people upstairs into the personal spaces instead of to the family spaces. When there are kids in the family, this can lead to alienation. Creating a strong focus that leads people to the community areas helps to alleviate this problem. If the first thing you see upon entering a house is the kitchen, you will want to eat all of the time. Moreover, everyone who comes to visit will end up staying for dinner! Forewarned is forearmed! Divert the eye to a different space and you divert their actions.

This is part of the secret of the success of the Victorian style of home, where the back door of the house led right into the kitchen. This is where the children would enter after school, and Mom could get a snack into their growing bodies. She also guarded the back staircase up to the bedrooms, so she knew who was upstairs and for how long. Many modern houses have lost this feature, and it has led to a fragmentation of the family.

Another factor in formal front entrances is the overuse of angular banisters. Later in the section on the nature of

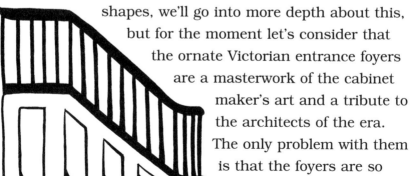

shapes, we'll go into more depth about this, but for the moment let's consider that the ornate Victorian entrance foyers are a masterwork of the cabinet maker's art and a tribute to the architects of the era. The only problem with them is that the foyers are so excessively masculine that, every time a person enters, their body is screaming for the cover of the foliage. This is probably why the Victorians were so fond of those potted palms: They literally overstuffed their rooms with overstuffed furniture.

These incredible complexes of angles set the body on edge. Those angles are just too close to the claws that we carry in our ancestral memories. When the same angles were surrounded by the extra cushiness of Victorian femininity, it worked. The problem is that modern tastes go for more sparse environments. It becomes very important in highly angular entrances to soften them by draping tapestries over the banisters using plenty of curved patterns. Weaving silk vines or even mini-lights between the spindles is also effective. So many houses today are owned and run by women that it's only appropriate that the entrances reflect their feminine personalities.

Issue Seven. Spaces that are Orderly and Accessible. Allowing clutter to build up in corners, block stairways or doorways, can be caused by a variety of issues. Often a lack of visual focus will set it off. Sometimes undue stress being placed upon one of the family members can also bring it on. We had a client who instinctively blocked the entranceway to her office by placing a coat-rack on the back of the door, so it couldn't open completely, slowing the energy down, resulting in clutter-filled the room. It was in reaction to a home that was otherwise open and sterile. There was no other place in the entire structure where she felt nurtured and safe. The house was so excessively Yang (open and bright) that she created the complete Yin polarity (dark and cushy) in her office.

Generally, you don't want the main energy pathways like hallways and staircases to be blocked. This is why your life becomes cluttered, stagnant. Unblock, reorganize, get those strong focuses in place, use a bright picture, mobile or chime to bring more energy into the area. Make especially sure that there is nothing behind the door, preventing it from opening completely.

Long hallways with too many doors coming off of them represents the opposite problem. Energy moves too quickly down the hall and doesn't blend well. This is one of the things that cause the downfall of the huge apartment complexes known as the housing projects. They contained long, straight hallways with doorways flush to the wall. Anyone who has walked down a long hallway like this with children knows that, by the time they are halfway down the hall, the children have run to the end. Why? Because children are more sensitive to these energies! All the people who have walked down this hallway have left trails of magnetic particles. The Chi travels along it as quickly as it can. The children are propelled by that energy.

The problem is that everyone who comes out of the apartments into this stream is propelled down the hall in the same way. Chi moves most productively when it can gradually weave its way along the trail, much like a meandering stream, picking up energy here and there, dropping some off as it passes through. In older apartment houses, doorways were recessed into the wall causing dips and cross-currents to slow the stream down. There might be a table or chair in the hall, as well as some pictures jutting out in relief, possibly with reflective surfaces to create light pressure to cut across the flow. As a result, when people stepped into the hall, the energy of the other tenants came to them. The energy flow was gentler, and they were more inclined to stop and talk with their neighbors, take a package in for them, and feel a sense of community.

This is often a problem when a teenager's bedroom is at the end of a long hall and they become isolated from the rest of the family. Hanging a crystal outside their room helps increase their interaction: Mirrors or pictures behind glass along the walls or at the end of the hall bounce or slow down the flow of Chi and encourage communication between rooms.

Issue Number Eight: Safe Havens From the World. Letting excessive light and noise sources (natural western light, automobiles and general passing lights and sounds) into the living spaces indiscriminately causes problems.

There are all kinds of pollution. In traditional Feng Shui this is Sha, which is another way of saying disruptive Chi. Sha is basically molecules of healthy energy that have been damaged by natural or man-made pressures until they are no longer healthy for humans or their furry or feathered friends. Sha causes disruption and difficulties with relationships, stress levels, and health. Don't let these disrupters flow unrestricted into the residence.

There are two basic strategies, best used together: Stop it from entering your space, and repair the damaged molecules and energy that do manage to enter. There's a number of ways of keeping it out. One is simply to block Sha with a physical wall, trees, or curtains, and so on. Another way is to create an energetic flow that will divert the undesirables. This is most easily done with mirrors. It's helpful to realize that mirrors reflect other kinds of radiation than solely the visible spectrum.

If you have noise in the form of inconsiderate neighbors, barking dogs, or general negativity from an overbearing building, placing a few small mirrors facing the offenders can be quite effective in overcoming the negative effects. How is this accomplished? There are actually a couple of functions at work. Simple, consistent light-pressure coming from a few mirrors is enough to set up a counter flow to divert the energetic stream coming toward your space. Now keep in mind that just because there is a potentially problematic structure near you does not mean that you are being harmed by it. For instance, if you are on a hill, and the problem, say it's a power line, is downhill from you following a parallel valley, the disruptive energy may be tracking away from you, following the path of least resistance. You might be able to see it, yet it might have little or no affect on you.

On the other hand, it's possible for problems quite distant from you to have a negative influence, if the geography and the qualities of light are such that the disruptive energy is flowing in your direction.

You Have to Guide Energy Where You Want it to Go

If those power lines are quite distant but

slightly higher than the property, that may be a problem. Additionally, if they are to the west of the house that may also be a problem. Light coming from the west, traveling as it does through a thinner, more de-ionized atmosphere has a lot more push to it. This would not be as much of a problem if the power lines were to the northeast, where the light wouldn't push the charge towards the property. Patterns of energy develop at ground level, but with some basic light-pressure, you can divert it around your property, just like diverting a stream of water with a dam.

The other factor at work here is information. Light is information. Remember those fiber-optic cables! In the same way that we respond to the light-pressure from a person's eyes when we look up, because we feel someone looking at us: People will respond to the feeling of the pressure of the mirror. In the case of barking dogs or noisy children, the noise tends to carry back to the house from which it emerges.

As we mentioned before, we had this exact case: We had barking dogs directly across from our office. During the warm weather the dogs were left in the yard all day long while the owners stayed inside with the air conditioners on. Every time a child would run by, those dogs would start barking. Well, we consult on the phone a lot, and our conversations are all tape-recorded for the convenience of our clients, so barking dogs on the tapes could be a problem. Two small mirrors placed facing the dogs were all it took. Suddenly, the owners started hearing their dogs for the first time. We were bouncing the noise back to them. They started bringing the dogs inside more frequently.

What happened next was especially nice because while we were bouncing back the noise we also bounced back the 'ugly' (imagine what the yard looked like after being trampled by dogs day in and out). The next thing we knew the sod truck came down the street, all the junk in the yard was carted away and a new lawn was put in. Now it was too nice to put the dogs in, so they bring them around to the other yard, where they can't see the children running past. Peace now reigns in the neighborhood for the price of two little 5-inch mirrors.

Amazingly this technique works right through walls. Remember the concepts of modern physics! Mirrors bounce other kinds of vibrations beside visual. Noisy neighbors next door or downstairs don't realize how noisy they are. Place a mirror with the silver face toward the problem. Yes, we mean point the reflective part towards the wall, floor, or ceiling. Don't worry, you can cover it with a picture. That way your friends won't come over and ask you why your mirror is backwards, (although it is a great starting place for an interesting conversation). The pressure of the mirrors will make the neighbors aware of how noisy they are and give them a sense that someone is hearing them. Pointing a mirror at a place in your yard frequented by trespassers is another way of giving them the feeling that someone is watching. Remember, it's just light pressure, but the body's electrical system is designed to react to it. It's subtle but effective.

A woman who attended our lecture series placed a large mirror under her bed facing down toward the bedroom of an outrageously noisy couple living downstairs in her apartment building. She was accustomed to hearing them fight loudly, but the night she placed the mirror, the couple had a screaming fight of frightening intensity, followed by sudden silence. After that, she heard nothing at all from them. A week later she checked in on them to make sure the wife was still alive. (She was). People are often unaware of how much noise and negativity they create until it's reflected back to them. Shifting the energy with the use of a reflective surface can bring issues to a head and allow them to clear out like a volcanic eruption.

Now, the other thing to do is to repair the damaged energy. This is where chimes that make beautiful sounds, plants that restore the oxygen, refracting crystals that make lovely colors and mobiles that dance beautifully with the wind, are all useful.

Issue Nine: The Voices of the Doors.

Doors that stick or squeak are a sign of poor communications in the house or building. Interestingly, if the doors that squeak are those on the exterior of the building, then the communication problems are occurring between the occupants and outsiders.

However, if the problem doors are all among the interior rooms, then the communication problems are among the inhabitants. So keep an eye out for where the "eeks" are squeaking. We used to say that it seemed impossible for a family with teenagers to not have some noisy doors, but then we found families where the squeakers were among the adults. Well, guess what? In some families, the children may be more mature and well-balanced than the adults! That's the key behind why a door gets noisy: Balance.

Every time a person goes through a door and pulls it closed, they tug on it and affect its balance. If the energy of the person is peaceful and balanced, then they transfer a balanced, sensitive, and firm energy to the door. It then swings easily and evenly. But if a person is unbalanced, due to a poorly placed bed or desk, where the aura becomes lopsided, then this imbalance is transferred to the door. It swings back and forth a little too hard, grinds into the hinges a little too heavily, wears off the oil, and the next thing you know it goes "Squeak", just like a mouse. It's no wonder we don't like that sound! When this continues the problem gets worse and worse until the whole frame is involved, and then the door begins to stick. Now communication is stuck. That door resonates to your energy and then reflects it back onto your aura.

You also do not want doorknobs to interlock or bump into each other. This causes a situation where the people are always "butting heads" with one another. The doorknobs are something you grab with your hand. Hands relate strongly to the nervous system and to communication. Anyone who doesn't understand that obviously has never had an extended conversation with an Italian. Ralph's Mom would make him sit on his hands every now and then (probably to save the glasses from being knocked over) and he would sit there silent, unable to speak without the expressiveness of his fingers. The knobs become programmed by the charge of the people. If your hands are daily handling doorknobs that are suffering concussions every day, this transfers into the nervous system and speech centers.

Obviously, it's important to maintain those doors. Always keep an oilcan handy. Be prepared to change a door for one that fits the space better. Always keep an eye open for where the doors are a problem. They'll tell you who in the family or work force is having a problem with communication or accessibility to resources.

Chapter Eight
A Colorful Code
The Power of Hue Over You

The way people react to colors is due to a mix of physiological, sociological and spiritual factors. What works in one society does not always work in another. Likewise, the knowledge that has come out of the mystery schools often needs to be adjusted to apply to modern tastes. What we present here is our own color theory drawn from personal studies and experience.

What is helpful to remember about the differences between the Western and Asian systems of color theory is that in the West, the favorite planets generally are Jupiter and Venus, which are expanders, and relate to luck and luxury. From the earth both have a blue tone. For the Chinese, the favorite planets are Saturn, a pale yellow planet that is the stabilizer, and Mercury, the silver planet that deals with commerce and children. We might say that, culturally, the difference is a focus upon possibilities versus responsibilities. Surveys have shown that the favorite color of Americans is blue, while their least favorite is yellow. This highlights yet another difference, which necessitates the adjustment of systems when practicing Feng Shui in the west.

GOLD and SILVER, for our needs, are not properly colors but rather metals related to the Sun, and to the Moon and Mercury. Gold is quite distinctly the glow of the Sun (Yang), and the warmth of the heart. The mutability of Silver can relate to the off-white of Moonlight (Yin) and the watery quality of emotions. When silver goes towards the highly reflective, we touch upon the energy of Mercury and the ability of the mind to reflect the exterior world. When we go to the soft, luminous silver we're projecting the feeling of the Moon, and the need to reflect emotions through empathy and sympathy. The real significance of these two metals (when used in design) is in their reflectivity, or in other words, their ability to translate and transmit light. Use them to balance Yang and Yin, both in interior décor and when you wear these metals. You can balance these polarities in your physical body.

RED is a primordial color. It activates our energy, our senses, our adrenals and our appetite. Our attraction to it is as basic as the newborn baby's attraction to the nipple that means food and survival. Red is the color of Mars, as well as blood. The eye will always go to red first, and it stimulates the aggressive side of our natures. It draws Yang energy towards itself. The activator! It attracts only positive energy. A problematic corner can be deactivated by placing a red dot under the point of the angle. It pulls the energy towards itself. Use red in "activity rooms" but avoid it in resting areas. However, red does inspire passion, so variations of red in small touches can add "activity" to the boudoir. Be careful about using red in the kitchen if anyone in the family has a problem with their weight.

YELLOW is the central reference point for the eye due to the yellow quality of sunlight. The large pixels at the edge of the eye react best to the gray shadows of evening. So the contrast of yellow and black are the extremes of the eyes' range. After red, this contrast is the single biggest attraction for the eyes. Yellow relates to the planet Saturn, the bastion of conservatism, compression, duty and responsibility. Yellow is America's least favorite color. It promotes maturity, restraint, and serious action. The very structure we rely upon! It is the appearance of reality. Yellow is the color of acquired knowledge, so it makes a good choice in an office or study space.

GREEN relates to Mother Earth herself. The Chinese value green jade over all other stones because it promotes harmony and serenity, in the same way that the garden of nature bestows these gifts upon us. The greens are soothing, sustaining, and speak of the abundance of the Earth. It is a sexy color, sensual, and tuned to satisfaction. In the West, green is the color of money. The sustainer! Green is easy to add to any environment through the use of plants. As living things, plants add energy and harmony to any space. Green touches in the bedroom add a sensual and balancing effect.

OFF-WHITE relates to the Moon, the nurturer, the touch of emotions, and is associated with Ivory, which the Chinese prize for its constancy and ability to be carved and colored and shaped by the human spirit. In Chinese society, where the most-respected planet is Saturn, the responsible, the Moon's polarity, the emotional flexibility and resilience of Luna is highly valued. The Chinese have a saying, "In life, you need soft lips and sharp teeth." The lighter tones of pink, green, and blue are the other primal colors mixed with the Moon energy. These various tones relate strongly to adapting these energies to nurturing, home, and human needs. That's why they're so popular in homes with young children. We have overused white in our environments. Where there's no color there's no emotion.

Use this for accents and woodwork. Avoid doing whole rooms or worse, entire houses in this off-white.

PURE WHITE in Western society is seen as a color for wearing in hot weather and as a symbol of purity, and cleanliness. It also relates, however, to sterility and the absence of emotions. It also relates to modern hospitals, places that carry a difficult association for most people. The absence of colors in pure white, besides reminding us of bleached bones, as a decorating scheme has the liability of adding no color to our auras. Thus they create a space that is low in nurturing and rejuvenation, especially if used in western-facing rooms where the light tends to already be more stripped of ions that the rich morning light of the east. The Asian cultures use pure white for mourning, and thus it carries a difficult societal connotation. The reason for that comes from their fear of the white fungus and molds that can attack their principal food crop, rice. White is a "cool" color, so it's not a good choice for any room in which you would like to feel cozy or nurtured. Use it sparingly or your spaces will take on a "clinical" feeling.

BLACK in Western society is seen as a color of mourning, of the night, as seriousness, and deadliness. Generally, it doesn't have a good connotation, although its sinister side does explain a bit about its popularity for fancy evening attire. In Asia, it's very popular and is related to water, which in turn relates to money. In a society that is based upon rice as its central grain, the blackness of the soluble minerals at the roots of the rice plants are understood to be the wealth of the Earth in reserve.

In Western society, with its heavy dependence upon grains such as wheat grown in relatively dry soil, black is seen as the absence of light, the growth of fungus and cankers that attack the roots in overly wet conditions, the dangers of the unknown, and the fear of the dark. It draws everything to it. While red attracts only dynamic energy, black absorbs all energy. Extreme use of black can rob you of your energy and let "black" thoughts and emotions dominate. Black touches here and there allow for the development of your intuition. Think about this both in environments and relative to the colors you wear.

BLUE is one of the three colors of love. Where pink is the color of romance and red is the color of passion, blue is the color of service to your loved ones. Blue is related to healing and beauty. It's the blue sky, the tranquil sea, and the clear eyes of a baby. It is another cool color. As America's favorite color, we often find blue in the bedroom, but it should be avoided if you're planning on any kind of warmth or passion there. Blue resonates with the bladder and kidneys, the organs most related to the emotions of fear and anxiety, at least when they're low energy. When they're high energy the kidneys relate to energy and the bladder to forgiveness. Many people are drawn to blue when their kidneys are feeling overstressed, a common experience in this society of coffee, cola, and too much time spent bouncing along in cars. Use touches of blue in spaces that require cool heads, or in rooms that get unusually hot. Blue can be used in a kitchen to balance the heat and to cool the appetite if you want to lose a few pounds.

LAVENDER, like the herb of the same name and the crystal amethyst, promotes clarity of thought, sobriety, and chastity. It's a high vibration, and like purple, has a spiritual tone to it. It relates to the asteroids and to the willing server without a personal agenda. The color we define as lavender can be any value, but it's essentially the equal blend of blue and red which takes you to purple, then add some white for purity, and we call this lavender. This is the color of chastity because it's the midpoint between passion and devotion with a little purity thrown in for good measure. Avoid this color in adult bedrooms. It can be used in bath or powder rooms and in the bedrooms of very young children, but be cautious. Sometimes early programming is hard to overcome. You'll want to plan ahead if you want grandchildren someday!

TURQUOISE and other forms of electric blue relate to Uranus and the energy of sudden, liberating change. As such, it's a color that needs to be used with discretion, since it tends to destabilize situations. It's the color of the revolutionary, the change agent and is useful when things need to be "shaken up". The turquoise crystal often has a high metallic content as well, and this energy is useful for boosting business or pulling an area of your life out of the doldrums.

PURPLE is regarded by many cultures as the color of spirit or the divine. It contains the red of passion as well as the blue of devotion, so it carries the message of both. The deeper the shade, the greater and more profound it becomes. As such, it carries power through belief. It relates to Neptune. It's the color of the believer. It can be used in adult bedrooms if the shade is strong and deep because it contains the passion and devotion without the white of purity. We like the shade to lean more to the red end of the spectrum. It's also a regal color so it can be used wherever you want to feel like royalty. Combined with gold accents, it is the perfect color scheme to counteract the drain caused by too many bathrooms in the financial sections of the Bagua.

BURGUNDY is the combination of red and black and is extremely Plutonic. It relates to the deep passions of the human body, and the primal drives to reproduce, burn away, and then reemerges anew from those ashes. Whenever a color is combined with black to create a deeper tone, it strengthens its intent, its mystery, and it further addresses the human issues of polarities. Use this powerful color as an accent to reinforce your power and strength and as a reminder that transformation ultimately leads to greater rewards.

BROWNS and TANS hearken to our long association with horses, leather harness, and animals as helpers and food. As such, it's an intimate color that has the potential to work in a supportive role to other colors. But brown also speaks of the wisdom of the natural world and the inner knowledge of the body in its ancient and complex design. The dark browns are Saturnine, and create structure and restriction. As trees stabilize the ground of the Earth, brown grounds and stabilizes our environments. In recent years, since the development of laminates and plastics, we started to see spaces with little or no brown in them. Without brown's subtle reminders, bills don't get paid, homework doesn't get finished, work assignments are overdue. While darker woods can be oppressive, lighter brown woods encourage us to be responsible. The most important aspect of color is how it affects people in their living spaces. A strong color will set off activity within a specific organ. Too much stimulation can overstress that body system. That's why balance is so important. Personal associations with certain colors should not be underestimated. For example, people who work in hospitals often don't like the color light green, similar to their work clothes. They especially may not like it in combination with red. On the other hand, while blue can be cooling, the startling blue that reminds you of a lover's eyes may be just what you need to raise your spirits when you walk into the room. Life in its rainbows of diversity is that complex.

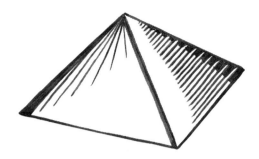

Chapter Nine

The Powers of the Earth

What's Hiding Under Your Home?

What happens when a building is constructed across an old road or an animal pathway? Pathways evolve through animals following the stream of electrical energy emitted by a crystal ridge in the surface of the Earth, usually an underground stream where forage is more succulent. As the Earth shifts in her daily rotation, the flexing and grinding of these crystals emit a piezoelectric charge. After a period of time, this ridge of minerals becomes imprinted with the electromagnetic fields of the animals. For instance, we worked with a house that was divided diagonally by a wolf path. Those wolves may have been gone for 50 years, but their energy pattern remains. Besides separating the house into two halves, its influence was found inside the home in very interesting ways. The owners kept buying sheepskins and they gravitated to this interior pathway. The house cats slept along the same pathway due to the feline's odd attraction to exciting currents, and the lady of the house, through her hair and her intense gaze was becoming increasingly wolfish in appearance.

The solution included using images of wolves in stone and glass, placed along the path as outlets for the energy. Unexpressed energy will find an outlet, often through the inhabitants. In another house, a powerful deer path bisected it and the woman who lived there took on that look of a deer caught in the headlights and became very fearful of confrontations of any kind. The solution for the owner was to get several large crystals and program them with her own energy. This is done by first soaking the crystals overnight in a bowl of pure water containing a high concentration of sea salt in order to clear them. Then the owner held them in her lap for half an hour while focusing on her intentions for her home; to have harmony, happiness, and prosperity. This infused the crystals with the person's program. Then the crystals were placed along the path to reprogram the underlying pathway energy.

Yet another house was built over rodent-infested farmland. The family had taken to collecting cute little stuffed mice and groundhogs and such. There were hundreds of them all over the house. The woman of the house had gotten increasingly "mousy" since living there, which was a major departure from her normal personality. We suggested that she get some images of wolves to keep the little critters in line.

We also have to deal with the pathways that we lay down. The power of the stream of particles at busy entranceways and pathways is often underestimated. Sitting or working where one's back is exposed to the energy left by walking feet is sure to result in either an underused desk or a messy work area.

What if that pathway is a road, and it points directly at your house? All of the cars coming down the street are carrying pollutants. The cars may turn, but the Sha continues traveling onto your property in a broad sweeping arc. The part of the Bagua that it hits can be a clue to the types of stresses that occupants live and suffer with. What if the house is at the bottom of a hill? Beyond the basic free radicals that flow down the slope into the property, remember about the molds, pollens, fungus and bugs that are carried along with the rain and the breezes that follow the grade of the land. All of that can end up in your living room and on your lap. Think of Chi as flowing like a stream of water and plan your house so it doesn't get its feet wet.

Everything Comes to a House at the Bottom of a Hill

The best solution for these kinds of external problems is to shape the land with mounds of dirt, planted with bushes or trees. Placing boulders can also be helpful. It's helpful to think of this energy as a flood and treat it like flowing water. As such you're better off creating curved barriers to allow the flow to be diverted to the sides, away from the building. When you create a straight wall, it needs to be higher to accomplish the same thing.

If you're in a situation where you can't remold your garden, fall back on the "smoke and mirrors". In other words, the "magic". Place mirrors facing out and chimes between you and the offending Sha. Cover the windows with plants and highly reflective curtains for the night. Do whatever you can to divert the problems, and do a lot of it!

Some Places Shouldn't Be Built On

The Significance of Directions

While we'll often hear that the best direction for the front door to face is south. What is often left out is how doorways facing the other directions affect the household. When we speak of directions here, what we mean is "What direction are you facing looking out of the building from your front door?"

There are several nice things about the Southern-facing house. On an ergonomic level when placing the beds, it is much easier to place the head of the bed towards the north. This is the healthiest direction for the body to sleep. On a more esoteric, level the southern door faces the solar, lunar, and celestial energies moving along the ecliptic (this is of course reversed in the Southern Hemisphere). Because these paint a complex pattern of energies on the face of the building, this position most easily serves the diverse needs of all the residents. It's the most potentially fulfilling, and typically, the most physically warming. Since the front of the house is painted with so much cosmic energy, it becomes highly energized, and everyone who looks at the front of the house sees and feels that quality. When the front door is opened that energy rushes inside.

The northern facing door is cut off from these spiritually and emotionally active energies from the Sun, Moon and Planets and instead, plugs into the Stellar vibrations of the deep night. Difficulties often seem to pour into such houses, and it's a good idea to find ways to bring southern energy into and through the house, from other doors and windows. The north is a direction that relates to knowledge seeking, and as such, is quite suitable for a school. Most Ivy League schools have their oldest buildings facing north. That's the main reason they're covered with ivy, a shade loving plant.

The eastern-facing house is programmed by the rising Sun. It promotes the sense of self and is great for the young family. It actualizes the individual, creativity, and all aspects of starting new projects. Couples have to be wary of the eastern-facing front door because it promotes the individual over the partnership. In those cases it becomes important to draw light into the house from the southwest and west to reinforce sharing. It's also wise to activate the nurturing and partnership sections of the Bagua in every room (the far right-hand corner #5, and middle of the right-hand wall #7, when standing in the doorway looking in). Also, place pictures of the couple and family as the first focus in the busiest rooms.

The western-facing door has the power of the setting Sun and is excellent for the couple since it supports personal completion through relationships, and affirms the collective needs. The family with a western-facing door has to watch out for the children never wanting to leave home, because they become so invested in their relationship to the family. It can also promote such a sense of serious commitment that injecting some fun and humor into the environment might become necessary. They also have to be careful to avoid litigation since the west is the direction of balance, and the scales of justice can be invoked. As long as partnership is married to fairness, the western entrance works beautifully.

The intermediate directions are combinations of these influences. The southeastern doorway activates the individual, but in a generally more self-satisfying way, due to the additional warmth of the southern Sun. It's not unusual for southwestern-facing houses to be passed down through several generations. This happens because the family believes in shared enterprises, they become invested in the relationship, and the southern direction permits for greater satisfaction for the members. The northeastern-facing door often results in an up hill battle for the residents about issues of personal initiative and creativity, while the northwestern-facing door often results in challenges about relationships with others. Challenges do not have to be negative things. The northern facing door of a school is an accepted challenge that potentially benefits all that enter there. But there are times when challenges are best avoided, and that's when the choice of the front door is critical.

Now is a southern-facing front door facing oncoming traffic from a cross street better than a western-facing door that is more protected? Probably not! The direction of the front door determines a great deal about how the building relates to the greater cosmos, but the house still has to deal with the neighborhood. That's why the three most important things about a property are location, location, and location. You can choose to designate a different door as the formal front door. After all, it's not like it grew there. But it must be done completely. The walk should be shifted, the house number moved, the mailbox relocated. The other entrance needs to be minimized and the traffic redirected.

Another factor that is often ignored is the direction that a person is facing when they're working, either standing or seated. The energy of the Sun, Moon and Planets go right through buildings. Why else do our radios work inside? If a radio signal can go through the walls of a building, how powerful is the signal from a planet? A desk that you sit at, facing northeast, will yield a much different result from one facing southeast. On the other hand a person is not a building, and some people will do better facing towards a quarter of the compass that's not viewed as kind for a front door. Looking at a person's Astrological Natal Chart will give us clues as to which direction (and which energy) they are facing. Your particular muse may be to the North in your chart, and maybe to the southeast. In any case, experiment. Turn your desk around, work for a while, and see what the experience is like. Do you make fewer typos? Do you get more work done? Don't assume that the direction doesn't matter, because it usually does.

How are you sleeping? In other words what direction is your head facing when you lie down in bed? Generally speaking the head of the bed is healthier in the north, northeast, and northwest. In a pinch it can point east or west. What you want to avoid is the head of the bed being along the south, southeast, or southwest wall. We've seen many cases of clients suffering from anxiety attacks, ungrounded fears, physical illness, and sleep disorders because they were sleeping with their feet pointing north. The pressure of the electromagnetic energy flowing south from the North Pole brushes the human aura during sleep. The lymphatic flow, with which the intuition is closely linked, flows down with the direction of gravity. If it brushes from the feet towards the head, all of the anxiety that's carried in the lower body is carried towards the chest. With the feet facing north, the natural flow of energy in the body is disrupted and the general wellbeing is gradually upset. For those with a severe health challenge, two of the best things they can do for themselves are to point the head of their beds towards north, and keep all kinds of electrical appliances and wires away from the heads of their beds. Even for a healthy person, this is a good strategy.

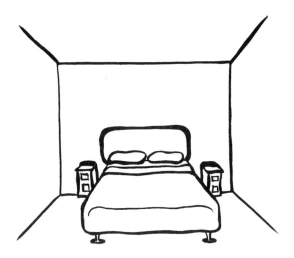

Chapter Ten
The Stars of Home
Cosmic Common Sense

Here we're getting into some deep waters, some really
fancy dance steps, with the application of Location Charts.
If you're not comfortable with astrological symbolism or
computers, or you haven't spent a lot of time looking up at
the night sky, you might want to put on some waders and
float over this chapter. We're not saying to skip it, but just
read it lightly. Most practitioners would consider Location
Charts an advanced technique. Even though we routinely
employ it, Location Charts are not in every practitioner's tool
bag. But we figure you have to start someplace.

A note about astrology: There have been a number of
times in history when there has been both prejudice and
persecution of Astrologers. It's helpful to realize that
throughout history many of our greatest natural
philosophers have been Physician-Herbalist-Astrologers.
Every major religion on Earth seems to have a strong
astrological heritage. When we look at the designs of the

great national capitol cities, including Washington D.C., we find that they all include significant astrological symbolism. In fact, in their stone and bronze work the public buildings and monuments of Washington contain more astrological references, including many complete horoscopes, than any other major capitol city on Earth.

Most of our greatest cities have been designed using some sacred geometry, with their streets and important buildings aligned with celestial directions. The triangle formed by the Washington monument, the White House, and the Capitol Building mirrors the triangle formed by the Royal Star Regulus, and the Sacred Stars Spica and Arcturus. Within this triangle is the constellation of Virgo, which is considered the ruling sign of America's capitol city. The great Egyptian pyramids are arranged in a pattern that reflects the constellation of Ursa Major, the Great Bear. This same constellation is carved into the face of the Mormon temple in Salt Lake City. In mentioning these few connections we have only touched the surface. From this foundation we can only suppose that any prejudice against astrology comes out of ignorance and fear. This negativity was, in part, triggered by the infiltration of Europe and America by sham fortunetellers and con artists. It shouldn't extend to highly trained and ethical practitioners of a great art that has served humanity well for eons.

Among the true mystery schools, it has long been the custom to not entrust sacred knowledge to those not prepared to cherish it. The original purposes of astrology were more related to the placement of buildings, and the forecasting of agrarian cycles, than to forecasting the future of individuals. With any great tool such as Feng Shui or Astrology, we have to be aware of what purposes it serves. For the individual Astrology can let you know where you are in the sequence of time. What lesson you're in the midst of and what lessons are coming up. In other words, it really is all in the timing. Astrology is a specialized knowledge of ancient lineage, on a par with medicine and law, and like those fields it has many specialties, and it's only as good as the knowledge, skill and integrity of the practitioner.

The special way we're using it here is to describe the pattern of the person's aura. We're looking for the individual strands in that paint brush, so we can more accurately recognize the pattern they paint on their environment. We ask that you use this technique, together with all of this knowledge, wisely. Putting that serious stuff aside, this is a fun technique, its easy to learn and its remarkably useful.

Following the first section, on using location charts, is a brief description of the planets and the astrological signs in relationship to Feng Shui and the other Earth Arts. This is your basic esoteric alphabet. If you're not familiar with the signature of the planets, this will give you a foundation that will prove useful. Maybe you're wondering why there's a section on Western Astrology and nothing on Chinese Astrology. The truth is out. We're from the West, not China, but we work with both systems. However, since we work in the West the challenge is to make the knowledge accessible. There's an incredible gracefulness in the Chinese system, and a remarkable precision in the modern Western system. We use both.

At its core, Asian Astrology is based on the planets, so the Location Chart technique for finding your personal planetary lines, is philosophically, right in line with it. Also, the Chinese Astrologers have interpreted the meaning of the planets a bit differently from their Western counterparts. Our descriptions of the planets definitely incorporate a mix of those two traditions.

This technique, Location Charts, is an extremely ancient system that was revived in the West due to the development of modern computers and their incredible calculating capabilities. It's at the core of all of the major astrological systems. So while the reference points are Western, the technique is universal in nature. We have used it extensively, and it's an amazing mix of science and mysticism.

The reason this technique re-emerged in the West is that Western civilization has a great command of geometry that can be traced back to our tradition of working in stone. Materials like granite and marble make excellent instruments for making and recording precision measurements, such as the movements of the Sun, Moon, Planets and Stars. That was an important purpose of great stone circles like Stonehenge. Probably the most famous of the many circles that dot the world, Stonehenge evolved over many years of celestial measurements and through the successive replacement of its monuments with others made from more durable stone.

These stone circles are computers for the practice of the three-dimensional astrology that is the original form of this technique, the Location Chart. It was this long tradition of precise geometrical mathematics that opened the doorway to the technology that has transformed our lives.

From a Feng Shui perspective it's helpful to remember that stargazing has been an important part of every major spiritual tradition. Determining the correct placement and door angle for a building or sacred site and in the process connecting Heaven and Earth has always been among the most basic and practical purposes for Astrology. The Western cultures have been blessed with a stable landmass. Having long-established reference points allowed us to fine-tune the geometry of celestial movements to a high art. Among the results were advances in global navigation, another was scientific advances, and yet another was this technique, Location Charts.

A Location Chart is most correctly described as a personalized Geomantic compass. It precisely reveals aspects of an individual's personal relationship to their environment. It does this through showing the unique pattern of planetary energies that are imprinted on an individual human aura at birth. The actual chart we use is calculated by a computer program and appears as a circle surrounded by planetary symbols, or glyphs, and crisscrossed by lines.

It shows the personal pattern of energy each person paints on their space. It's as unique as a snowflake or

The Mountain Top of Earth

fingerprint. The perspective is different from a modern astrological chart, being much simpler. The chart's center point is you, whether it's where you were born or the center of your current home.

The way in which the Location Chart works offers deep insight into the motive forces inherent in Feng Shui. This is how you create a Location Chart: Imagine that you're standing on a high mountaintop facing south. You're able to see the complete horizon in a great circle all around you. In the Location Chart, the outer circle is the horizon, and the cross hairs at the center is where you're standing on the mountaintop.

To your left, watch the Sun just peeking over the eastern horizon. Look overhead at the southern sky, and you'll see the planets spread across the sky like jewels. There's silvery Mercury just leading the Sun, and chasing flashy blue Venus. Overhead is red Mars, and setting in the west are cold blue Jupiter and pale yellow

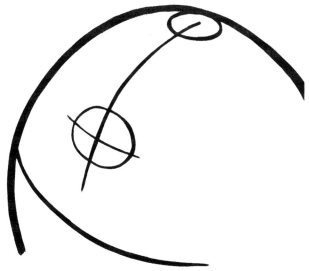

The Location Chart has a Different Perspective

Saturn. Leading them, just above the Western horizon, is the almost full Moon.

There is nothing but some gaseous atmosphere and asteroid dust between you and those great transmitters of energy. The planets' electromagnetic fields wash over the Earth in great continuous waves. When a baby is born the patterns of the planetary energies imprint themselves into the living human energy field like hot colored fibers wrapped around a plastic balloon. They create permanent colored impressions. The aura may later change its shape, expand, shrink, or deform, but those imprints are still there under all the accumulated experiences that are piled on. The pattern has a continuing influence on how energies flow through the individual into their environment.

Remember to visualize this in three dimensions around you. When we live in a house, we paint the environment with our energy pattern. It becomes the repository of our energetic history, and it literally reflects back on us, reinforcing our sense of identity and wellbeing. This pattern shown by the Location Chart aligns itself with the true directions of the Earth. So when aligning the printed chart we use true north rather than magnetic north. That means you need to find out the magnetic variation from true north in your area and adjust your compass for the difference.

Visualizing three-dimensionally, notice that the globe of your aura fits itself into squared-off, nonsymmetrical buildings all the time you're inside them. The shape of a space influences the shape of the aura. Conversely, if you have blockages in your personal or professional development, you'll project these onto your living spaces, oftentimes in the form of clutter. Conversely, if the shape of your space doesn't allow for full expression of all of your energies, areas of your life will be restricted.

The Location Chart is simple in concept but profound in its applications. The printout is a circle with a cross in the center. At the top is North, just like a compass rose. Around the edge of the circle are the symbols of the Sun, Moon and planets. From each planetary symbol lines extend through the center. To use the chart very simply, we take it to the middle of the overall living space and lay it on the floor. Then we align the top of the page with true north.

Now imagine where the lines extend out and through the house. This shows where the planetary energies are active. This can be done for each floor of the house. Remember these are projections of your energy, the pattern that the planets imprinted in your aura at birth. While the planetary energy is active along this whole line to a width of three to four feet, we've found that it tends to be strongest in the direction of the symbol since this is the original source.

What does this knowledge do for us? There are two basic ways in which we usually use it. First, it will tell us

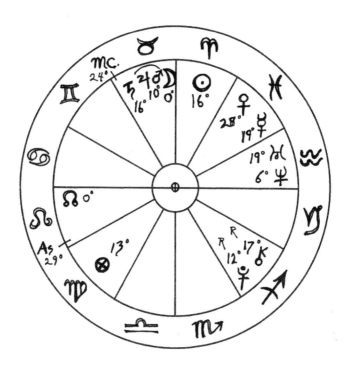

The Natal Horoscope

what direction we need to face to most fully actualize a part of our lives. If we want to increase our sense of beauty, we might face our favorite chair towards our Venus point. This is the direction Venus is shown in the chart. For example if Venus is found due south in your Location Chart, when you face south you are addressing your Venus energy. If we need to increase our sense of discipline, we might place our desk so it faces our Saturn point. If we need to expand our possibilities, we would place our desk so we sat facing our Jupiter point. We might face our exercise bike towards our Mars line, to boost the energy available for a good workout. This is where our description of the planets in the next section will become really helpful.

What this technique does is face the aura energy centers (Chakras) at the front of your body directly at the energetic pattern that you are painting on your environment, related to that particular part of your life. It reminds you to focus on that area of your life. It makes you resonate to that planetary theme. What you resonate to, you attract to your life.

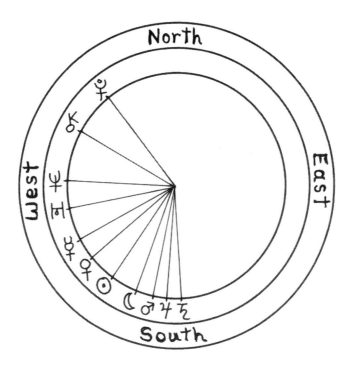

The Local Space Chart

The second way to use a Location Chart is by highlighting what behavior is happening along the pathway of the line. In other words, if you took a can of spray paint and marked out where each line went from the center of the house out to the exterior walls, you would find that along each energetic corridor that planetary energy is very active. Where this is especially helpful is to show the underlying reason for a problem, when there might be no obvious flaw in the design from a purely Feng Shui perspective.

Here are some examples. The bed is well placed commanding the door, there is not too much light, and no oppressive features. The husband can't sleep there, and when he does, he has nightmares. His Saturn line runs down his side of the bed. The planet Saturn is representative of the father and has a tendency to be very stiff and unyielding. From our discussions with the husband we find that his relationship with his father was very problematic. Every time he lies down on that line, he vibrates to that energy. In the other bedroom is his Jupiter line, related to generosity and good health. The best solution is to change bedrooms. A second solution is to place a very tall and stiff-looking piece of furniture between him and the center of the house. It would need to be where he can see it from the bed. This way, it can play out that Saturn energy, so the energy doesn't have to play out through his body.

Another example: A couple is arguing consistently, but always in the same place in the kitchen. The space design is harmonious, but the husband has parallel Mars and Mercury lines there, leading to temper tantrums that dissipate quickly. The wife has Sun, Venus, and Moon lines running through the same area that make her react emotionally to the assault to her femininity. The result is that he gets over the explosion immediately, while she remains wounded for a prolonged period and doesn't really communicate the issues well. The solution is simple. Put some bright red apples (Mars) in a silvery bowl (Mercury) to pay off that Mars-Mercury energy. There's no need to play out her energies, since they are perfectly comfortable in that space. Then eat in the dining room, where the lines for both of them are more harmonious!

Yet another example: A woman can't sleep later than

5:00 a.m. in the morning in her own bed. However, her romantic experience of the space is positive, and in fact very exciting. There's nothing in the ergonomic design that denotes that. But running down the length of the bed are her Venus and Uranus lines. Great for exciting and inventive sensual experiences, but that Uranus line is generally too stimulating for sleeping, and tends to make the person light sensitive.

After the client rejects the solution of moving the bed (big surprise) we suggest that she hang a colorful mobile with lots of turquoise and silver or aluminum over the bed. These are colors and materials that relate to the Uranus energy. By letting the vibration transmit itself through this moving object, it does not need to express itself through her. After hanging an Indian medicine woman's pouch that she already had over her bed, she had to buy an alarm clock so she wouldn't oversleep.

When we go on consultations we bring a Location Chart and Astrological Chart for each resident. Every individual has unique qualities that are demonstrated in their chart. While planetary energies tend to work in a certain manner, they vary from chart to chart in terms of their strength and effectiveness. It takes some astrological training to analyze this variation in depth, but this added perspective isn't necessary to use Location Charts effectively. The reason is that the planetary lines are only an issue when they cause problems, and when that's the case, they're definitely strong. A deeper understanding of the astrology offers a wealth of insights about the issues hiding beneath the surface, and can offer an even more exact analysis that can lead to precise solutions. Computers are a major reason for the growing use of Location Charts. It can take eight to ten hours to make these calculations manually. With a computer that process is reduced to minutes.

Let's examine the characteristics of each of the lines. You'll notice that the outer planets have more text devoted to them. Here's the reason for that: The inner planets are more personal, and the outer planets are more impersonal. When these patterns develop in our spaces the personal energies rarely give us a problem, but the impersonal energies oftentimes activate difficult programs. So to resolve those issues takes a deeper knowledge of the players, so you can maneuver yourself around them more effectively.

☉ **The Sun.** This is your spiritual program and essential energy, the overall theme around which your life revolves. The Sun line is where you feel most centered, creative and warm. This is good for a bedroom, office, or family room. It's a good place for your easy chair and your favorite reading spot. Face the Sun in your chart to warm your heart, spark your creativity, enhance your sense of self-protection, and assert your position as the center of your own life.

☽ **The Moon.** This represents your emotional program and your need to nurture and receive nurturing. It's an adaptable part of yourself that adjusts easily to changing conditions and needs. This is a good activity area for nurturing, emotional connecting, sleeping, and that cushy couch you like to hide away in. This is the perfect place to nurse a baby. Beware, things move on a Moon line. This is the first place to look for your missing keys. Facing the Moon encourages your willingness to be emotionally sharing, receptive to others, comfortable, and conscious of personal gain.

☿ **Mercury.** This represents the talent for conversation, thought, and the ability to find a common ground between yourself and others. It's a very personal energy and has a youthful quality to it. This is the line for the telephone, working with communications and the hands, as well as for consulting. It's also a good place for parking your bicycle. It's inclined towards short-attention-span theatre. It's hard to sit on your Mercury line for long periods of time. You always find yourself sitting on the edge of your chair, ready to go somewhere else. When you face Mercury your ability to communicate goes into high gear; it increases your mutability, flexibility, and willingness to encounter new people. This is a very good direction to face for business.

♀ **Venus.** This relates to your sensitivity to beauty, and the ways in which you express love and wish to receive love. It also concerns the types of friends you like around you, and the environments where you tend to find your friends and lovers. It also shows how you commit to partnerships. This line is social, artistic and loving. It's good for sleeping and harmonizing diverse needs. It also serves well as a conference and mediation room. This is the place to eat chocolate and to be self-indulgent. Think hot tub. It's also the place to talk with people that you really like talking with, either on the phone, or in person. When you face your Venus line, your beauty is enhanced. Your artistry and diplomacy become an active part of your life. Love just comes to you more easily.

♂ **Mars.** This shows how you physically express yourself. This is how your physical body likes to get things done. It can relate to physical strength and aptitude as well as grace. It's the line for high physical activity, exercise, games and loving, but not necessarily sleeping, since the person gets energy when they lie down to sleep. It may be too ego-centered and activating for you to unwind enough to sleep. If there are chronic arguments in the house, watch for connections between the residents' Mars lines in the hotspot. Mars is one of the two lines that we especially watch for in a consultation, because of its potential as a troublemaker. The trick is to play the energy off with a single bright red object where the person can see it, or a lot of water imagery to cool it down. Facing Mars boosts your physical energy, your dynamic personality, and your willingness to encounter new challenges. People suffering from chronic fatigue can make use of this Mars energy as well.

♃ **Jupiter.** This relates to your ability to plan your future and develop a philosophy about life to guide you there successfully. It also shows your feelings about travel and the ways in which you expand your life. This is the line for expanding. It's the preferred area for entrepreneurs who need to look towards the future. It's athletic and thus good for an exercise room, although not good for the refrigerator, since it could expand your waistline! Generally it's a good sleeping line, but tricky. If you go to bed feeling good, Jupiter expands that feeling, but if you go to bed worried or in pain, Jupiter expands that instead. Like Venus it has a tendency towards self-indulgence. This is a good line for the home office, and for your health. When you face Jupiter your luck comes alive along with a certain foolhardiness. You are able to more easily tap into your visionary side, and the future becomes a much more interesting place.

♄ **Saturn.** This shows how you deal with responsibility and your willingness to forgo your personal wants for the sake of the group. It's the energy of structure and the skeleton, and as a result it has a tough reputation. It's not a soft and cuddly line in any of its manifestations, but it's very responsible and can be very restricting, ambitious and reserved. This line is good for an office if your work relates to practical issues or if you need to project a formal appearance. Saturn projects a stiffening energy, so sleeping on a Saturn line tends to make a person feel mature, sometimes oppressed, but usually stiff, especially in the knees. It's a good line if you want to be taken seriously, since it makes you seem older and more mature. Not a great line if you didn't have a great father, because it keeps reinforcing an energy that doesn't work well for you. If you had a great Dad, it could be a great line for you. Facing your Saturn brings out your serious side, makes people take you more seriously, and encourages you towards conservative choices.

♅ **Uranus.** Here we get to the planets that were discovered in modern times. They can't be seen without a telescope. Uranus is the planet of revolution and innovation. Whenever important new inventions come upon the scene Uranus is a player. It will show how you innovate and rebel. It will show how you use change effectively in your life. The Uranus line seems to draw computers, televisions, electronics and other types of mass technology. This is the other line we always watch out for, because since it's exciting, disruptive, and inventive, it's not very good for sleeping. The typical sleep pattern on the Uranus line is that a person will have no problem falling asleep, but a couple of hours later they will come wide awake. Then they'll toss and turn for the rest of the night, or until they go and sleep on the couch.

Since the Uranus line attracts electrical devices, if the bed is there it's not unusual to find the bed stands cluttered with radios, boom boxes, the occasional fax machine, and the obligatory phone, with answering machine built in. The unexpected happens on a Uranus line, and in the bedroom that means not sleeping. It's a rather impersonal, intellectual energy, so it's not especially good for the love life, unless its runs parallel with a more emotional line, such as Venus or the Moon. If you face your Uranus point, expect the unexpected, because it will alter your normal viewpoint and make the unusual more attractive to you.

♆ **Neptune.** The energy of this planet dissolves,

relaxes and intoxicates. It has an illusionary and meditative quality. It will show how you connect with this quality within yourself. This line is a great place to sleep or unwind, since things just naturally dissolve here, including egos, consciousness and resistance. Things tend to disappear on a Neptune line by hiding in plain sight. This is the second place to look for your keys. Unless your work is extremely dependent upon the imagination, this is a difficult line to work on. On the other hand, it's a good place for spiritual communing. This is a good direction to face for meditation and imagination, since it brings you beyond your personal needs into the arena of the visionary. Face this way to activate your intuition and compassion.

♀ **Pluto.** This is a secretive, powerful, sexual and transformational planet. It shows how you use power and the ways in which you are aware of power. It deals with your secret self and your relationship to the deeply transforming powers of society. This is a great line for a massage room or any type of deep healing space, since Pluto likes to get beneath the surface. It can be a very isolating line, but people are drawn to sleep on a Pluto line when they feel the need for profound change. If one person in a couple is sleeping on a Pluto line they can feel alone even when they're in bed with the other person. It makes for very intense sex, with a life-or-death quality to it, but issues of sex as power can become a factor. Face your Pluto when you need to plumb the depths of a mystery, manage a difficult situation, or transform an aspect of your life.

There are five other major bodies in the Solar System that we often use. They include Chiron, a planetoid between Saturn and Uranus, and the four largest asteroids in the asteroid belt. We're not discussing them here, but we're mentioning them to illuminate the idea that there are many aspects to this art.

While understanding the astrological signs is not necessary for using Location Charts, they do represent the basic cycle of life upon which the Bagua is based. So here's a simple description of the 12 signs with a tilt towards how they relate towards the environmental arts. A note for the astrologically literate: In our description we use the traditional, visible rulerships. By that we mean the planets that can be seen with the naked eyes. Three-dimensional astrology is very obvious, practical and down to Earth. From that point of view the evolving demands of the changing seasons are the priorities of the 12 signs. So now, we're going to discuss the western astrological signs in relation to Feng Shui.

♈ **Aries.** Springtime begins with the Mars-ruled Ram, dynamically masculine and bristling with life. This is the newborn baby fresh from the mother's womb, red, raw and all potential. It's the sprout bursting through the crust of the soil, with the genetic structure of the mighty oak tree impatiently waiting to manifest. It's your ability to be self-centered, creative and bold.

The Aries energy in the chart is great for starting things but a little light on follow through, so it makes for great salespeople but poor administrators. Aries tends to sudden anger, but it so lives in the present that it doesn't carry a grudge. Aries doesn't tiptoe into situations but crashes into them. New people, new situations, new ideas are all food for the Aries soul, making them stronger and more anxious to see what the next day, the next hour, the next moment will bring.

♉ **Taurus.** When the leaves fold out with the fresh green of the fullness of Spring, the Venus-ruled Cow, adorably feminine, comes into her own. This is where the baby suckles at the mother's breast and receives satisfaction. This is when the bounty of the Earth makes good on her promise, and the child is bathed in beauty and love and establishes their tastes and standards that they will carry throughout their lives.

While Taurus is luxury loving and comfort inclined, they have no problem working hard to attain those goals. Their goals are often those possessions that give them pleasure, those foods that satisfy their tastes, and art that pleases their eyes. This is the security of the early Spring, and money in the bank is the security that the Taurus energy seeks. Taurus is patient, enduring, and inclined to move slowly, but they also can be stubborn and resistant to change. After all, if you're in the clover, why would you want to move?

Ⅱ **Gemini.** When the birds and insects begin to dart about, it's the time of the Mercury-ruled, boyishly masculine Twins. This is when the child gains the gift of language, and little hands can grab what they want. Kids and games are the province of this sign, as well as the ability to communicate and converse. This is the ability to explore the neighborhood and become part of a close group, speaking the special dialect that shows that "I'm like you" and that you belong.

The Gemini energy is inclined to a short attention span. Quicksilver changes and molds itself to the situation, reflecting and illuminating it. That's the Gemini energy. It's lightning quick, nervous and changeable. It's sparkling wit, mischievous comments, and outlandish jokes with a naughty flavor. Just when they're about to get into trouble they change faces, charming their way around you and safely out of danger.

♋ **Cancer.** As the first fruits appear upon the trees, enter the Moon-ruled and profoundly feminine Crab. This is where the gathering begins, where we hold onto resources for our children and our future. This is the need to be needed and the seat of emotion. It's the tender interior hiding behind the crusty exterior. It's a cautious sign because it now has something to lose. It's protective and mothering, adaptable and deep.

The Cancer energy gathers and holds onto their possessions, creating an ever more comfortable nest. The Crab sidles into situations, moving towards what they want by rotating around it, gradually pulling that object of their affections into their own orbit. Receptive to the maximum, emotionally profound, deeply needing love and someone to love, the Cancer energy will pour out tender loving care. These people invest their emotions, and they expect a return upon their investment. Experience has taught them how to spot a likely prospect.

♌ **Leo.** In the heights of the Summer when the heart sings is the time of the Sun-ruled and grandly masculine Lion. The fruit is there on the tree, so just reach your hand out and grab it. The weather is hot and the blood rich with nutrients. This is a time of passions expressed, creativity and courage honored. It's dramatic, generous, and regal. It's a time for basking in the Sun and enjoying the spontaneity of life.

The Leo energy has no trouble being the center of attention, accepting applause and taking their bows. But Leo can also be counted on for a good tip, a gracious smile and a hearty handshake. They're not inclined towards innovation, but prefer the tried-and-true, popular routines. There's no one better as a leader, not because of their far-reaching vision, but simply because they're so good at gathering attention and support for their cause. The Lion can be fearless at defending their territory and ferocious when protecting their tribe. High drama and grand theatre are the tools they employ and they handle them better than any of the other signs.

♍ **Virgo.** With the late Summer and cool nights comes the work of the Mercury-ruled and purely feminine Virgin. It's the time for harvesting the grains to sustain us through the Winter months. It's the time for hunting late at night under the full Moon to harvest the wild creatures. It's time to put everything in order and in its place, to be industrious and attend to the details. This is the time to pass on the basic skills, and in the process, prepare and refine the next generation. It's the time to demonstrate the skills that establish your place in the society.

The Virgo attends to details, focuses on the task at hand, and puts the needs of another ahead of their own. It's not that they're selfless, they just take they're mission very seriously. Virgo is the energy of the craftsperson who works through a step-by-step process to attain perfection. It's a logical, practical energy that adjusts to the situation but doesn't lose track of its mission. Humans are the first concern of the Virgo, but with catlike detachment they can seem aloof to their emotional needs. With deft flexibility they weave themselves into other peoples lives, while maintaining their integrity and tracing an often circuitous route to their goal.

♎ **Libra.** As the leaves turn into a blaze of colors, we come to the time of the Venus-ruled and gracefully masculine Balancing Scales. As the Autumn foretells the coming of the Winter, the making of fair and equitable partnerships becomes paramount. Negotiation and diplomacy are vital skills for establishing connections that will allow all members to contribute and receive satisfaction through cooperation. This is the time of commitment and ritual. It's the time to create harmony.

The Libra energy is always balancing, and so direct action isn't its preferred method. The creation of beauty is one of the aspects of Libra, and the need for symmetry is essential to its nature. The feeling that anything done is better done in cooperation is the hallmark of the Libra ideal. While they desire harmony, they have been known to spark a fight, just so they'll have something to hone their negotiating skills upon. Justice is their cause, and interminable bargaining is their cost. They're committed to relationships and will spend endless time and attention establishing the rules by which the game will be played.

♏ **Scorpio.** As the green world dies back and the bare branches emerge, the Mars-ruled and deeply feminine Scorpion makes her entrance. This is where the partnerships move forward with power and stealth. This is intensity and intention. This is commitment and obsession. This is the dying back in preparation for rebirth, with all of the transformational power that process involves. This is deadliness and delight. This is the power to soar above and to dive deeply into life. This is sharing power, with all of the intense emotion that risky endeavor entails.

When Scorpio enters the game, it plays in earnest, and all of the other players become a little bit more intense, a tad more obsessive, because Scorpio will tilt the balance of power in their own favor given the chance, and it shows. Scorpio will share the power, but wants a hand in setting the terms, and will negotiate every point when there's something really at stake. Scorpio needs to feel the profound depths, the extreme heights, and the forces in action. Scorpio gets bored with inaction, insipid decisions, or games without stakes. Scorpio likes commitments that matter.

♐ **Sagittarius.** On the verge of Winter, the old growth is cleared away, leaving a pristine clarity, and the Jupiter-ruled and enthusiastically masculine Centaur Archer appears upon the fields. With visual clarity comes mental clarity and the time to plan for the future. It's the time for storytelling, for teaching ethics, and for travel and adventure. It's the connection between making voyages and developing a better perspective. It's the ability to use the bow to hit distant targets and the mind to grasp distant concepts. It's the optimism that comes from visualizing the future.

Sagittarius can span the distance between what it wants and what it gets in amazing leaps because it believes it can. Such unabashed optimism deserves the luck it enjoys, because there're no small parts in the Sagittarius personality, only big hearts, big mouths, big voices, big muscles and big ideas. When they leap beyond the limitations that harness lesser mortals it's because they've taken the time to look beyond the daily grind into the world's philosophy, theosophy, commerce and travel. It lets them see where they want to be and that's where they go.

♑ **Capricorn.** With the coming of Winter and the hard frost upon the land the time of the Saturn-ruled and sternly feminine Sea Goat comes. These are the times when the walls of the village and the walls of your house become your primary protection against the harshness of the outside world. This season begins with the shortest day of the year. The needs of the group overshadow the needs of the one. This is where your labors over the previous year are demonstrated. This is the prosperity you are able to exhibit before your community, showing your social position and respect for authority.

The Capricorn energy puts the social before the personal, the political before the emotional, and the career before the family. Working hard to fulfill their responsibilities Capricorn believes in the collective purposes of society. They are resolute in their social pathways, and their favorite direction is up. They expect to work against some obstructions and will often choose the path of most resistance. They can be formal, reserved, conservative and yet surprisingly ardent in matters of love and passion. Mating is, after all, a social commitment, and they take all of their social commitments seriously.

♒ **Aquarius.** In the deep Winter and the coldest time of the year comes the Saturn-ruled and remotely masculine Water Pourer. Now the resources are not the green plants growing on the land. They are the food stores and supplies tucked away in the cellars of the families that make up the community. The need to network among your friends and acquaintances to locate and trade those resources is now essential. The hierarchy established in the previous month now serves as a guide for navigating this network. However, in the chaos of the marketplace, inventiveness and innovation may overturn the social structure.

The Aquarius energy bestows the big view and the wide picture. It's more concerned with the needs of the whole tribe than the demands of the individual. This is the reason for their reputation for detachment. It's the shepherd energy, and they are most content when in the midst of that controlled chaos, moving their herd along with an occasional tap on the butt or head. Seeming the most placid of signs, Aquarius can go from their patient watching mode to electrical and disruptive action in the blink of an eye. It's an innovative, at times eccentric, and definitely alternative energy that needs to disrupt the status quo from time to time.

♓ **Pisces.** As the days lengthen, the snows melt and the energy hidden within the Earth rises. This is when the Jupiter-ruled and dreamily feminine Fishes appears. The last produce of the old year, battered by the cold, is dissolved and made available to the new seeds. This is the time when belief in the coming Spring is the only thing that carries you out of the stagnation of Winter. This is the time of cool nights and deep dreaming, when the imagination and

169

spiritual sensitivity is strongest. This is the time of shared beliefs, compassion for the common good, and an awareness of the suffering of the less fortunate among the community. This is where we seek communion with the Divine.

The Pisces energy believes and often suffers for their beliefs. They dream and invite others to join along. If their invitation is denied, they'll turn away and dream alone, waiting and hoping. This gift of imagination allows them tremendous empathy, and they feel another's suffering as if it is their own. They can invoke great vision, including sparkling details, and their unquenchable belief is often an inspiration to others. In a world where image is everything, Pisces is Empress.

It's from here that we enter the time of the Ram, the new spring, the birth of the new sprouts, and the return of the warmth upon the Earth.

We use Location Charts because they show the overall patterns that the family is painting on their spaces. The charts are not a substitute for a good grounding in ergonomic design and the nature of energy pathways. On the other hand, working with it consistently does seem to increase the effectiveness of the intuition. As we become aware of the lines and learn to recognize their look and feel in various places, we find we can identify their indicators when they appear in an environment.

Another facet of this tool that is fun to know about, even though we're not going into it too deeply here is that cities and towns also have Location Charts, based on their incorporation or founding date. We find that their prosperous main streets are on Sun lines. The fanciest shopping is on Venus lines. The garages and car dealerships are on Mercury lines. Due to the nature of duality, both the churches and the seediest bars will be found on the Neptune line. Look for the herbalist shops, healing centers and health food stores on the Jupiter lines.

These are ancient systems in a modern context, and they are best learned in application. Doing some additional reading about the nature of the planets as they're used in astrology is helpful. It's a specialized technique that can be applied with tremendous depth and subtlety.

Chapter Eleven
The Geometry of Survival
What Shapes Say to You

Feng Shui is an art, and as you practice it remember that artists need to develop a special view of the world. Artists need to actively study nature in order to recreate it using the symbolic images that make up the language of design. A primary part of every artist's training is figure drawing. This is based upon the belief that all shapes in nature are found in the human body. A command of these shapes bestows a firm grounding in the universal language of design. It also satisfies a practical and essential need for the artist, the ability to portray the image that which people most often want to see: Other people!

Much of the power of design is based upon visually recognized shapes programmed into the body at primordial levels. Understanding this visual language is vitally important in the work of Feng Shui. In part, where modern architecture has gone astray is through the over reliance on the two-dimensional renderings of blueprints. This focus on the two-dimensional visual sense excludes the significance of the other senses that are three, four and five-dimensional in nature. Height plus width plus depth equals three dimensions. That completely formed object in motion is the fourth dimension. Objects moving through space forming repeating, often curving patterns create the fifth dimension, time. It's from this complex construct that vibrations emerge, which in turn creates color. Since we react to all of these dimensions, shouldn't our homes be designed with all of them in mind? That's what Feng Shui is all about!

The combined power of curves, color, and movement are embodied by a woman wearing a red dress, walking across the room.

When she appears, most of the people, men and women alike, will turn to look. Often the women look first, then the men follow suit, then the women smack the men, and the men say, "I was just looking where you were looking!" Sure! Why does this happen? Because the autonomic nervous system is aroused by the combination of curves, red, and motion! Why else do advertisers employ so many images of women and babies? Those curves and dimples relax our defenses and throw those primal switches from run to cuddle.

It's helpful to understand the relationship among the three levels of our physiological selves. Interestingly enough, while we were created in the image of God and Goddess, we seem to have created computers in our own image, and we can learn a lot about ourselves from their design. In our daily lives, we're continually dealing with the relationship between the conscious mind and the autonomic nervous system. The autonomic nervous system in turn has two parts, the sympathetic and parasympathetic systems. While the conscious mind may pride itself on being in charge, it has little actual control over the sympathetic level (fight-or-flight) and virtually no control over the parasympathetic (rest and digest). Yet the three have to work together, and how well they cooperate has a lot to do with how well you feel day to day.

Their relationship is mirrored in the computer. The monitor screen represents our conscious mind, our window on the world. The RAM, or random access memory, is similar to the sympathetic nervous system that runs the fight-or-flight reflex. It stays busy interpreting and balancing the needs of the conscious mind and the primal body. It can be managed by the conscious mind, but generally it works automatically. Then underneath that is the machine itself, communicating in its own machine language. This is

The Computer was Created in the Human Image

the domain of the ROM, the read only memory, the parasympathetic nervous system, which is in charge of the rest-and-digest mode and the main processing that the user cannot change. It's the core personality, the most ancient design in your body. If you don't like the design of the processor, then turn in your machine, reincarnate, and try again. You can always hope for an upgrade, an advance in evolution.

Here are some key points about how the three layers of

your system cooperate. When "Windows" is up there on the screen, that's the conscious mind up and running. The lights are on. At that time you're centered in your modern, civilized mind, focused on where you left your car keys and where you have to be at 3:00 p.m. tomorrow, hopefully on time. But whether or not the conscious mind is occupied, down where we don't notice them, RAM, the fight-or-flight reflex, and ROM, the rest-and-digest mode, are online and running. These two subconscious parts of your system are focusing all of their attention on the moment-to-moment practical concerns of the whole body. Being so practical, they are very literal in their perceptions. That's why shapes and designs that might appeal to "Windows" up there can absolutely terrify RAM and ROM. The survival of the body is their Number One priority. In the presence of shapes that promote the wellbeing of the body, they become physically stronger. Confronted by shapes that threaten the wellbeing of the body they become weaker. Their programmed reactions continually affect our actions, outlook, self-image and emotions.

One of the most important factors at work is the interrelationship between Fight-or-Flight and Rest and Digest. If your body is tense or frightened, as when you're sitting with your back to the door or sleeping in a vulnerable position, your Fight-or-Flight system is active. It also means that the Rest-and-Digest will not function.

This is because all the available energy has to go to the all-important ability to fight or escape danger. If you eat when the fight-or-flight is running, the food lands in a digestive system that's not ready for it. The food falls through the system in chunks, damaging the intestinal tract, and over time destroying the body's ability to use nutrition. This reduces the overall vitality, the immune system, and the sense of wellbeing.

If you try to sleep in a situation that your body interprets as threatening, your ability to sleep and restore yourself is reduced. Then the health problems are blamed on stress. Sometimes the best thing to do is simply follow the instructions your feelings give you.

If you can consciously choose to feed, nurture, and rest yourself in environments that feel as safe and protected as you can possibly manage, you will be honoring the needs of your natural self. You will be also doing a tremendous amount to enhance your health and sense of wellbeing.

Let's look at this from another point of view. When your conscious, logical mind overrides your other programs by telling you that you'll get used to an uncomfortable situation, that 10 percent of your brain, which is what the sequential part of intellect represents, is trying to override the programs of the other 90 percent of the system. The friction that results is called stress, and this arises whenever people ignore their body sense. When you tell your body that physical feeling doesn't matter, the body doesn't believe you. Why? Because eons of evolutionary experience have shown the body that ancient designs know best. The body never forgets, even for a moment, the survival program.

There's a language in shapes. Why do we like round shapes so much? It's the contour of the Sun and the Moon! The circumference of a tree! But it's also the shape of the eye, the body and the breast. Our most basic programs activated before birth associate rounded shapes with food, life, love, and survival. For the rest of our lives, the sensitivity to round shapes will continue to command our most basic programs.

As we know, life is made up of polarities. The balance to the round is the straight line, and our eyes read those sharp angles as teeth, fangs and claws. In our environments, it's the exposed,

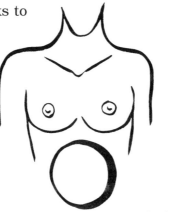

angular beams, and the external attacking corners that create stress in our bodies. That makes sense to our physical senses because it reflects the logic of how our personal world is constructed. Straight lines are Yang, and they form structures. Curves are Yin, and they form comfort.

The Shapes of Nurturing

The language of shapes explains the power of feminine beauty. The word aesthetic comes from breath, as in to "take your breath away." When you suddenly encounter overwhelming beauty, you find yourself breathless. The history of beauty in art is an ode to the feminine. The female human is the more diminutive, a Yin quality. Yet it's Venus, the supple and curvaceous who is our standard of beauty.

Let's consider the geometry of survival. Imagine being a desert nomad, tracking the seasons from the passage of the Stars across the Sky, and establishing a Solar compass to navigate the sands to the next oasis. The rising of familiar Stars herald the time to move the flocks to other grazing. You have sand and stones as a drawing board and reeds for your markers. Tough cord made

Breast and Claws

178

from gut is your measuring device. With a reed and a cord you can make two primary shapes, the straight line by drawing the cord taut, and the circle by using the reed as the center of a compass and drawing the cord with its marker around it.

With these basic tools and the shadows of the rising and setting Sun you can establish the Vesica Piscis which will show you true North, South, East and West. Knowing these four points is the foundation of navigation across trackless expanses and wilderness. Recognizing the changing angle between the rising Sun and true East is the foundation for the counting of days, and the creation of the calendar.

This makes the meeting of the Yin circle and the Yang straight line, the starting point for human geometry. They are the first two letters of the visual language that our body depends upon to navigate through life. This language is essential to the workings of Feng Shui and modern ergonomic design. The key is to recognize where these shapes exist in nature, so that when you use them in your environment, you'll know what to expect. Here are some examples of shapes in action:

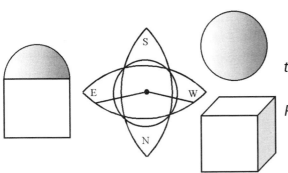

These are Some of the Basic Geomantic Shapes: Vesica Piscis, Sphere of the Heavens, the Cube of the Earth

During a consultation in a health-food store, the owner mentioned that she had a problem with slow turnover on incense. The rack was a horizontal row of thin dowels, six inches long, coming out from a backboard that the packages hung on. It had been designed to mount on a countertop, but the owner had fixed it to the wall at eye level. Every time customers looked at it, they got the feeling of fingertips moving towards their eyes. That made their heads turn aside. The stock below it on the wall was selling even more slowly, because one had to bend over to reach it, leaning into these attacking claws.

Here's another example: While teaching a workshop at a yoga center in the Winter, one of the participants, for the sake of comfort, wore her bedroom slippers. They were shaped like two little, quite realistic dogs. She was sitting literally at our feet, and whichever one of us was standing by her got distracted every time she moved her slippers. This is the instinctive reaction you have when two little dogs are coming at your ankles.

Yet another example: While shopping at a toy store, on a rack of hand puppets, we found one the size and shape of a New York City rat. Although it was soft and cuddly, whenever any of us caught sight of it in our peripheral vision, our body's reaction was extreme discomfort. No logic, no rationality could overcome the instinctive reaction to that combination of color, shape, and movement. While there was some discussion about buying it to use as a demonstration in our classes, saner minds prevailed.

A final example! The daughter of one of our students had a great deal of success by rounding off the sharp visual angles in the grammar school classroom where she taught. Through using chalk to change the shape of the board to a rounded-off rectangle and putting paper flowers on the protruding corners of cabinets, and so on, and soon the children's stress levels were so reduced in this rounded, nurturing environment, that their classroom demeanor dramatically improved. The difference was so marked that the other teachers noticed, and the practice spread quickly throughout the school.

There's a balance between stress and nurture that is determined by the needs of the space. A meeting room with a beautiful view may need some exposed beams to create tension to stop people from daydreaming away their day. Modern impersonal, angular lobbies of office buildings throw our bodies into the fight-or-flight reflex that our logical mind tries to override. There are more subtle threats that are keyed to primal shapes that have a history of danger, even in our more personal environments, such as that rat hand puppet, striped wall papers, exposed beams, and sharp furniture corners. When they appear in our surroundings we respond. Many people try to ignore or suppress the subtle chattering of the natural machine screaming out its program for survival. But there's a lot to be gained from listening, feeling its impulses, and valuing its advice.

The style of design and the nature of building materials have a powerful philosophical impact upon a society. As we create changes in our environment, our environment changes us. As the wind shapes the mountain, the mountain shapes the wind.

Chapter Twelve
Herstory History
Where This Art Comes From

Now that you have a few good "dance steps'" under your belt, let's sidle up to the bar for a cool drink and discuss some of the history of this art, Feng Shui. It's an ancient practice, either 2,000 years old, 5,000 years old, or maybe 16,000 years old, depending upon whom you ask. Honestly, its history is lost in the mists of time, but we can safely say that Feng Shui started somewhere between the dawn of time and the invention of the personal computer.

In China the lineage of Feng Shui is tracked back to the *I Ching,* that ancient book of practical and spiritual knowledge which has a recorded history of at least 5,000 years. But truthfully, even that book's formation extends further back into prehistoric times, making its first appearance as markings on what are known as Dragon Bones. Those are ancient inscribed ivory pieces found in tombs. It has been a favorite practice for herbalists to grind up these fossilized fortune-telling instruments, for use as part of their healing potions, because they are a wonderful form of calcium carbonate. But then some archeologists caught them at it. The practice has not entirely stopped, but at least the archeologists sometimes get a chance to read their markings before they go into some client's tummy.

Western Geomancy goes back to the great pyramid of Egypt, and that has defied dating. Ask any Indian scholar how long their system of Vastu has been practiced. "Forever" is a good answer. For as long as there have been humans on this Earth, the various forms of this environmental art have been weaving the human design into the arms of Mother Earth.

We're in a unique time and space today. The traditions of the pyramid builders, the cathedral masons, and the western mystics are all meeting the ancient knowledge of Asia in a remarkable example of East meets West. The playing field, or rather the dance-floor, spreads across the Americas, Asia and Europe. That knowledge, which has been cast aside in the rush for the new, is crystallizing into a powerful system strengthened by their collective synergy, based upon great traditions, and illuminated by scientific validation.

Humanity lives with this art all of the time. The secret codes and dimensions have been programmed into sacred structures in every culture, and thus imprinted on the people who use them. But buildings decay, timbers rot or burn, and even stones can eventually wash away. We practitioners are ever gathering up the threads of a sacred knowledge that is threatening to unravel through the vagaries of time.

So keep in mind this is our personal view of the history of this art of space manipulation. It includes Feng Shui, Geomancy and three-dimensional astrology. All three have blended one into the other, throughout time, around the world. If our rendition is different from others, well, we can only base it upon what we've observed and what we've woven together, as best we can, from the remnants of diverse cloths and logical application.

As the societies of the world established stable agricultural communities and roads to tie them together, leaders were charged with guiding the placement and construction of buildings, bridges and roads. The western title "Pontifex" denotes a high priest, it traces back to the words Pons meaning bridge, and Facere, meaning maker. The Pontifex was the maker of bridges. As we sail across our modern highway spans, it's hard to imagine the difference a bridge can make to a community. It overcomes the dangers of crossing a rushing stream with a raft overloaded with people and livestock. Yet as we cross a great river on these threads of steel, asphalt and concrete, there is still something magical about it, seeing the sunlight flashing off the water far below. Of course a bridge is more vulnerable to wind and water than most other structures, so knowledge of these forces is of great importance if you plan to span rivers with your dreams.

The primary study for these builders was to understand how to be in harmony with Earth. Modern society has ignored this, much to our detriment. There's an art to fitting buildings among hills and valleys. Is it in the lee of the wind, safe from the water pouring from the ground and falling from the sky? Is it aligned with the paths of the Sun, Moon and Planets, taking advantage of their energy? Ignoring these components when we place a building means denying ourselves the gifts of Heaven and Earth.

Following this route leads to a balanced abundance known in Asia as "the way" or the *Tao*. Taoism as a system of knowledge is very conscious of the feminine nature of Earth, her ability to respond, to be receptive and reactive. From Taoism came a consciousness of the power within life, Chi, with its two complementary parts, the two essential

energies at work in every situation, Yin and Yang. When the
energy levels of Chi degrade and become stagnant it
becomes Sha, static, free radicals. Great design consists of
attracting Chi and dispelling Sha, and each major school
goes about this in slightly different ways.

The *I Ching* is the foundational text of Chinese
philosophy. It represents the progression of the Great Circle:
The movements in the heavenly sphere. These are the yearly
transits of Sun and Moon through the bands of the Earth's
Aura, illuminating the sequence of changes that organize
Earthly life. It includes a complex numerology and system of
archetypes, representing the multifaceted aspects of Yang
and Yin, the Solar/Lunar component of Astrology. Such
knowledge was considered essential for the proper timing
and planning of farms, communities and the roads that
interconnected them. The I Ching is in a practical sense,
aside from being an oracle, an instruction manual for the
management of human life in a social world, useful for
peasants and vital for Princes.

The *I Ching* or *Book of Changes* is an integral part of
Asian culture. It has been a forum as well as a frequent
battleground for China's greatest philosophers, astrologers
and statesmen. The book has served many functions, and it
has been reshaped to fit the changing agendas of the
political weather. It's through their shared roots in the I
Ching that the various schools of Feng Shui establish their
antiquity, and pedigree.

The oldest is the Form School, which approaches this
knowledge with the intuitive and aesthetic senses of the
artist, naturalist, geologist and mystic. Consider the
methods of the Form School. In your mind, imagine
traveling across the land, choosing the sites for farms, roads
and towns. You would always be focused upon taking the
best advantage of the bounty of the Earth, and the warmth

of the Sun. Like an artist creating a balanced composition, it requires the ability to see the similarities between a geological structure and a primal power. Go out and see how a river path resembles a snake. Mountains look like the backs of dragons. The prevailing winds bend the trees in certain directions. Learn to read the signs of the land, sky and water, with both an analytical skill and intuitive, creative sense. Project the best site for a road, bridge, house, village, farm, tomb, or palace. Then feel how the Earth and her inhabitants respond to your decisions.

Mountains Are Rivers of Rock

To do that really well requires knowledge of geology, meteorology, plant biology, and chemistry, together with a fluency with symbolic languages and the nature of an artist. While this sounds quite sophisticated, the first time someone tells you that they can't get a relationship going, and then you see that their bed is crammed into a corner, with no way for someone else to get to the other side, the power of practical symbolism becomes very clear. Trust what you see and you won't need neon arrows pointing out the clues.

Although much of Asian Feng Shui can be traced back to Taoism, the core beliefs were recycled through the *I Ching*, and thus through Confucius. This was a watershed event. It's unfortunate that his name sounds so much like "confused" in English, because he did have a lot on the ball. In fact, Confucius is actually a title meaning "wise man", although at times we wonder about how wise he was, since he reportedly disliked and distrusted women. So when he became an influence on the I Ching, women were pretty much written out of the practice of Feng Shui and moved over to side with the cattle and other livestock.

That's where you can still find them in the current translations. It was from this strongly patriarchal background that separate, competitive schools of Feng Shui emerged. But the wheel has turned, and while most of the teachers who brought Feng Shui to the West have been men, the practitioners in America are, for the most part, women.

The Compass School built on the Form School's foundation of directions and carried it farther into the aspects of horizon-based Astrology.

Through the study of the synchronicity of the Solar System and the influence of planetary and stellar lines crossing the Earth, they developed their Geomantic Compass, or the "Loupan". How are Compass School, Geomancy and Feng Shui related to Astrology? Well, here are the nitty-gritty details. Astrology is Astrology is Astrology, even when it sometimes turns into a form of numerology, which the Chinese and Tibetans are inclined to do. This approach made them less dependent upon the exact planetary observations necessary for the Western and Indian systems. Fitting all of these various systems under the banner of 'Astrology' does mean stretching the definition a bit, but the starry arts have big shoulders: They can be generous.

While these hybrid methods are often good systems, they have a failing similar to that of the Form school: Lack of flexibility. The joke that many of us have heard goes: When you invite the Compass Man in, be prepared to move, because the only solution is to move the front door.

The Compass School was a natural adjunct to the Form School at the time it was formalized. First, you find the right place in the landscape to put the village using Form School methods, then you use the compass to align the buildings, to gain the maximum energy and good fortune from the interplay of the heavens and the landscape.

One small problem, though! These methods don't offer much latitude when solving a problem in an existing building. Of course, as practitioners, we could simply shake our heads sadly and say, "What a shame! You should have called me before you let your landlord build here. Do you have any strong friends with sledgehammers? You need to move that door over to the other side of the house. Otherwise you're never going to get that promotion, and your love life is going to stay in the dumps." While such a cure might be justified, there could be some logistical, not to mention legal complications. One can almost foresee Supreme Court precedents being established concerning a tenant's right to correct a truly horrible Feng Shui faux pas.

This brings us to the current evolution of the art, to the modern Mystical Schools that have come out of China during the Cultural Revolution. Feng Shui was one of the traditional arts that were put on the Red Guards' blacklist. It was in some ways more vulnerable than the other arts, because it was dependent upon the community for its very workplace, namely the public buildings, businesses, homes and tombs. It's kind of hard to keep your work hidden, when it requires you to travel around the landscape wearing long robes, and carrying arcane measuring instruments.

As a result, many of the practitioners migrated to Hong Kong, Taiwan, Singapore, and other places where they could practice their art freely, albeit in urban environments. So there arose a need for solutions that fit a different type of clientele. Then, as other Asian arts like karate, judo, kung fu and meditation traveled to the West, Feng Shui traveled with them. The modern Mystical Schools offer flexible, simple, inexpensive solutions that work. This is how they do it.

Over hundreds of years, practitioners of the art visited buildings, homes, temples and palaces and learned a great deal about what we call in modern industrial design, ergonomics. It's the conscious design of objects to comfortably fit the real dimensions of the human body. Ergonomics goes beyond the simple measurement of the static figure, into a study and understanding of the human organism in motion and reaction. It includes the sensory interaction of people with other people, colors and images, as well reactions to animals, plants, minerals, manufactured and natural objects, and the complex, technological environment society creates.

Very simply stated, we are actively affected by our world in ways that we typically are not aware of, yet our autonomic nervous systems depend upon this input and reacts to things we don't consciously see, based upon its ancient programming. These survival systems are directly keyed into our subconscious mind and override the conscious mind, activating muscles when they feel danger is present. This is why sitting with your back to the door creates tension. The conscious mind knows that there's no danger behind you, but the body knows that there might be. In your genetic history, in the codes programmed into your blood, your body remembers saber-toothed tigers creeping through the high grass. The tigers were there before, and they might come back again, and they love to creep up behind their prey. In the ancient past your body learned that, and it's not the kind of thing your body easily forgets.

In studying people's responses to their surroundings, practitioners saw patterns develop. Families with a stove facing the door were happier and more prosperous than those with stoves that required the cook to feel vulnerable. Our modern Feng Shui faux pas of placing stoves, a fire, against a wall, is to the body just like building a campfire next to a tree. Nonsensical! The tension of the cook, standing with their back to the door is transmitted into the food.

They noticed clutter in one part of a house had a different effect than when it was somewhere else in the room. These cumulative observations became a body of knowledge. Since the Asian Mystery Schools were working with an agricultural people, they put the knowledge into short stories that made it easier to remember. But of course, the stories didn't reveal the dynamics at work. Even in Feng Shui, there's such a thing as protecting the trade secrets.

All of the traditions developed rituals of intention and clearing for changing the energy in a space by using incense, smudge sticks, bells, bright colors, song and dance to lift up the energy and dispel the residue from past problems and pains. This is the purpose of the dancing dragons and fireworks during Chinese New Year celebrations. They clear away all the left-over negative energy of the previous year, so the new seeds can sprout, free from those past influences.

The modern Mystical Schools gathered the rituals together with the environmental secrets. A little friendly advice related to rituals. They need to be followed up by changes in the physical environment to be effective. The influence of most Feng Shui rituals will be written over by electromagnetic pulses from the Earth's rotation and shifts in the underground energy streams. The purpose of the ritual is to clear and ease the pathway for beneficial action, not as a replacement for the action itself.

This manipulation of energy could be called magic, but a 150 years ago, the idea of energy flowing through the sky or along the ground sounded like magic. Today we call it electricity and microwaves. It's been awhile since Mr. Edison lit up Menlo Park and Mr. Marconi grabbed hold of the airwaves, so we should be getting a handle on this by now. Energy flows, and we are part of that current. Astrology is very properly known as the science of effective energies because of its wide influence. Feng Shui is the science of responsive energies. We do things with our environment and the Earth responds.

Why do diverse schools form? Due to differing environments and building materials! China is a fertile land with many seismic tremors so the Chinese traditionally used bamboo, wood, boulders and paints to create their buildings. The Europeans endowed with a more stable, but less fertile land, cut stone and created diverse masonry materials, like the concrete of the Romans. India is a mix of both, fertile, yet stable. The Arabian world with its mix of desert and oasis, traces its ancestry to the Nile, and like the Europeans the Arabian history is carved in stone.

Remember the story of the three little pigs? The first pig built with straw, and the second one with sticks, which were both readily available, but a little short on wolf-proofing properties. The third little pig piled up bricks, and his house stood up to the huffing and puffing of the wolf just fine. It's not that straw and sticks are bad building materials. Straw bale houses can be comfortable, and energy efficient, and the islands of the South Pacific have a long tradition of houses made of sticks. The thing is that those two little pigs weren't very good architects. They didn't adjust their designs to fulfill their needs, and to fit their environment. Lucky for them the third little pig did! He understood that the key is fitting the building to the site, choosing your materials to suit your weather, and create designs that suit your needs.

The Western tradition of Geomancy sits firmly on the foundation of Plato's words "Let none ignorant of geometry enter here," and with good reason. Stone, the building material of the western sacred sites, is among the most labor intensive building materials imaginable. In a non-mechanistic age, those entrusted with its measurement were imbued with powerful religious and social responsibility. Any mistakes they made were extremely costly in blood, sweat and tears. The numbers on the compass that measure the sky tell us where we stand on the Earth but also where we are amid the heavens. The Western tradition has sought to describe this relationship with the precision of a cosmic clock. Some buildings keep better time than others.

All of the diverse approaches to this Art, no matter the time or place in which they evolved seem to share the belief that the Earth is a living community of flowing energies. Positioning yourself correctly in relation to those forces is essential to attaining good health, prosperity and loving abundance. Knowing how to find your best place has always been basic to finding your happiness. Use this knowledge with love, joy and compassion, and choose your place wisely!

About Us:
Ralph & Lahni DeAmicis

We're really very nice people, who work daily with ancient mystery systems, and do it pretty well. As professional Feng Shui Practitioners, Astrologers, Herbalists and Numerologists, we continually mix and match ideas, techniques and solutions to unravel the tangled knots our clients bring us.

Sometimes we feel like the Sherlock Holmes and Dr. Watson of the esoteric world, in that most of our consulting these days is for other consultants, who bring us those odd, over the edge puzzles that they can't untangle themselves

There are a certain advantages in having taken an extraordinarily long time deciding what we wanted to be when we grew up. It meant that we pursued extremely diverse professional lives, while deeply studying on a broad, esoteric front. This gave us the opportunity to apply these mysterious systems in many different applications. After a while, 30 years or so, this kind of experience adds up.

One result has been that we seem to be especially good at applying ancient knowledge to modern situations. From teaching hundreds of workshops and doing thousands of consultations, we've found ways of explaining these mysterious concepts in modern, social terms.

195

Part of our success as teachers comes from the unusual fact that we, right from the beginning, have always 'tag-team' lectured. We flow back and forth in our presentations, and while our senses of humor are not identical, they are complementary. So while we might be Sherlock and Watson in one part of our work, in a seminar, there's definitely a touch of George Burns and Gracie Allen.

With over a hundred published articles to our credit, both nationally and internationally, about a third of which relate to Feng Shui, we definitely have a hand in the literary world. We've lectured at most of the major Feng Shui conferences and have also lectured at the same level on Astrology and Natural Healing.

We're directors of one of America's largest Feng Shui programs, the DeAmicis School of Feng Shui. Our programs are available at multiple locations. The classes are taught by us, together with our team of personally trained seminar leaders. We also administer the DeAmicis School of Natural Healing. We offer classes ranging from introductory Feng Shui, right through advanced, professional seminars. We offer a wide variety of accessory classes as well, on topics like aromatherapy, crystals, kinesiology, dowsing and astrology.

Behind all of this, we're a couple of artists and scholars. We're business people and mystics. We're both born in the year of the Rabbit, which explains why we have 5 children and 5 grandchildren, and why we like to cuddle up together eating carrots. We live in a home filled with our original works of art, our family photos, and some really great Feng Shui. But we're always ready to move the furniture again for a good cause.

Ralph and Lahni DeAmicis
www.FengShuiandtheTango.com

The DeAmicis School of Feng Shui
Philadelphia, PA
Call 215-464-5149
www.FengShuiAndTheTango.com

Do you know how your environment is creating your destiny, shaping your attitudes and directing your future? This comprehensive training and mentoring program will place the keys to these particular secrets in your hands, so you can design your world to suit your needs. You can pursue this to further you own personal development or as a skill to augment your current livelihood. Or you can use this knowledge to establish your own successful career as a consultant in this ever more popular and valuable profession.

The DeAmicis School of Feng Shui offers you one of the world's most modern, comprehensive, and professional training programs, blending the traditions of East and West and covering the three major dimensions of this field, while maintaining a cohesive theme from beginning to end. You will be guided in your own life-design process, as well as in the consultation portfolio you will develop throughout the program. You will emerge from the school with all of the skills you need to design your own success and if you wish pursue a prosperous and effective career.

The core curriculum consists of 9 one-day seminars that address in depth the essential powers of Feng Shui and Geomancy, providing the student with the breadth and depth of knowledge necessary to practice these arts in a modern environment. Additional seminars are periodically offered on associated subjects to augment your command of the field. To begin you have two options. Start by taking the three-evening introduction, Feng Shui: Designing Your

Destiny. This helpful, insightful and entertaining series of classes is available at most Learning Studio locations. If there is no convenient Learning Studio nearby, you can instead purchase the Dynamic Feng Shui and Functional Feng Shui audio-tape sets. Listening to these and studying the booklets will give you the necessary foundation in the uniquely modern and effective approach that this program employs. Suggested reading: Feng Shui and the Tango in Twelve Easy Lessons by Ralph and Lahni DeAmicis.

Once you are familiar with the principles covered in the three-evening introduction, or the tape sets, you can enter the program at the next scheduled one-day seminar. There is no specific order in which the seminars need to be taken, but there are 4 pairs where one seminar builds upon the knowledge of the other, so we suggest you start with one of the seminars marked with a Star *. The overall format of the program has been designed to be easy and convenient for the student to pursue as well as reasonable in cost. The sessions are held on the second Saturday of every month, except, July, August and December. They begin at 10:00 AM. The essential materials are covered by 5:00 PM, leaving until 6:00 PM for questions and answers. Both continental breakfast and lunch are provided onsite. With this format, whether you're five miles away or five hundred it is convenient and easy to attend.

Experience has shown us that participation in one-day workshops on a monthly schedule, combined with taped lectures and an active mentoring system enhances absorption and command of the material while avoiding burnout and the confusion of over-saturation. Once a student has participated in a seminar they are invited to attend it again for simply the materials and meal charge. In this way students can explore other aspects of the subject and pose questions about issues that arise during consultations. The seminar location rotates between several area Learning Studios.

The faculty consists of Ralph and Lahni DeAmicis and their team of Seminar Leaders. This team approach allows the student to establish mentoring relationships with various professional practitioners. Ralph and Lahni are well known in the Feng Shui community for their modern and entertaining style, their broad understanding of the field, their highly effective systems and techniques, and their ability to pass on this knowledge in a practical and useful manner. Their Seminar Leaders are all professionals in the field, talented teachers, and thoroughly conversant with this international, humanistic and multi-media method of learning.

To register or for more information about the school, or Ralph and Lahni and their Seminar Leaders (including an extensive collection of their published articles), plus details about the international programs visit www.FengShuiandtheTango.com.

For additional information call 215-464-5149. Please note that participation in the overall certificate program is not required to attend individual seminars, although the pre-requisites are the same. To purchase books or tapes please call toll free 888-998-BOOK.

The Core Curriculum

- *Professional Tools for Unlocking Hidden Issues: Includes explorations of the Euro-Bagua and The Three Levels of Energy.
- Power-filled Techniques for Creating Change: How to Manipulate the Energetic Threads in the Universal fabric of Life.
- *The Secrets of Happy Homes and Rapid Real Estate Transactions: The Art of Moving In and Moving On. Where to Live and Where to Avoid.
- Empowering Business Prosperity with Feng Shui: Creating Success and Focus for Commerce. Turning Businesses Around.
- *Form Feng Shui: Crystals, Energy Clearing. Nature Spirits. Reaching beneath the Surface to Effect a Change.
- More Form Feng Shui: Discovering Earth Issues with Dowsing. Refining the Intuition. Discovering the Hidden Voices.
- *Modern Compass: Astrology. Five Stages Theory. Universal Symbols Used for Creating Powerful Tools. Recognizing and Using Archetypes.
- Ultra-Modern Compass: Local Space and AstroCartography Solutions. Sacred Power Triangles and Prosperity Directions.
- *Keys for Running a Successful Consulting Practice: How to Create Success for Yourself at Every Level.

Books and Audio Tapes from Ralph and Lahni DeAmicis

Feng Shui and the Tango in Twelve Easy Lessons
Why Feng Shui Works and How to Make it Work for You
A modern, practical book that helps you make Feng Shui a useful and effective tool for improving your love, money and health now and for the rest of your life.
216 Pages Soft Cover $15.95   ISBN: 1-931163-03-0

Power Feng Shui   Available Early Summer 2001
Filled with well-tested, highly effective techniques for healing today's ills, Power Feng Shui leads you step by step to the solutions. Each chapter addresses a major issue with esoteric and practical instructions. Subjects like eliminating clutter, planning a happy wedding, selling a house fast, clearing ghosts, supercharging your career, getting a good night's sleep and more. An entertaining, informative must have reference.
256 Pages Soft Cover $15.95   ISBN: 1-931163-05-7

Audio Tapes from the DeAmicis School of Feng Shui

1. Dynamic Feng Shui
Here are the foundation concepts of Feng Shui, including powerful techniques for creating change through tugging threads in the Fabric of Life. Here you'll find the in-depth essential Euro-Bagua, the three levels of energy and emotional color theory, western style.
2 Audio Tapes & Graphics Booklet $19.95   ISBN: 1-931163-10-3

2. The Essential Tool Box
Which objects unlock hidden issues, effectively manipulate Chi, and resolve critical issues? We explain how and why the tools work and how to use them most effectively.
2 Audio Tapes & Graphics Booklet $19.95   ISBN: 1-931163-11-1

3. Action Feng Shui

Imperative steps that immediately create beneficial change. Effective resolutions for a host of Feng Shui faux pas, with illustrative real life stories.

2 Audio Tapes & Graphics Booklet $19.95   ISBN: 1-931163-12-x

4. Financial Feng Shui

Empowering prosperity, creating commercial focus and success and revitalizing businesses. Secrets of happy homes and rapid real estate transactions. Moving in or moving on. Where to live and where to avoid. Clearing spaces of leftover energies.

2 Audio Tapes & Graphics Booklet $19.95   ISBN: 1-931163-13-8

5. Celestial Feng Shui

Modern FS Astrology including 5 stage theory and location charts and the universal archetypes used in energetic tools. The most esoteric module and one of the favorites.

2 Audio Tapes & Graphics Booklet $19.95   ISBN: 1-931163-14-6

6. Directional Feng Shui

The direction a door or a desk or a bed faces makes a difference because every compass point signifies something special. We explain the meanings of the directions and the differences between the front door and the main door. Includes Sacred Triangles, general and personal prosperity directions.

2 Audio Tapes & Graphics Booklet $19.95   ISBN: 1-931163-15-4

7. Romantic Feng Shui

The techniques for inviting love into your life and convincing it to stay. Essential Bagua secrets, ergonomic and color clues, and directional keys that unlock the spiritual pathways to Earthly love.

2 Audio Tapes & Graphics Booklet $19.95   ISBN: 1-931163-16-2

8. Challenging Feng Shui

The Essential Checklist. Solutions for universal challenges that often appear due to prevailing design styles. This goes to the core physical, emotional issues and shows how to improve them.

2 Audio Tapes & Graphics Booklet $19.95   ISBN: 1-931163-17-0

9. Evolutionary Feng Shui

What was Feng Shui in the past and what is it today? We explain how the diverse schools interrelate and when to use them? We share the secrets and systems you need to run a successful practice now and into the future.

2 Audio Tapes & Graphics Booklet $19.95   ISBN: 1-931163-18-9

10. The DeAmicis School of Feng Shui Complete Audio Tape Series

A comprehensive, modern, professional-level Feng Shui program. Encompassing the major schools of Asian Feng Shui, Western Geomancy and Modern Ergonomics. This includes all of the individual tape sets plus a comprehensive graphics booklet

18 Audio Tapes & Master Graphics Booklet $149 .99ISBN: 1-931163-19-7

Cuore Libre Publishing
Quick Order Form

Fax Orders: 215-671-8672 Send this form.

Telephone Orders: Call toll free 888-998-BOOK,
> Please have your credit card ready.

Email orders orders@CuoreLibrePublishing.com
Postal Orders Cuore Libre Publishing, PO Box 728, Bryn Athyn. PA 19009, USA

Please send the following books or tapes. I understand that I may return any of them for a full refund for any reason, no questions asked.

Item_____ Amount_____

Item_____ Amount_____

Item_____ Amount_____

Subtotal_____

6% Sales Tax PA residents only_____

Shipping_____

Grand Total_____

Shipping by air:
US: $4 for the first book or tape set and $2 for each additional product.
International: $9 for the first book or tape set and $5 for each additional product (estimate)

Name_____

Address_____

City_____ _____State_____Zip_____-_____

Telephone_____

Email address_____

Payment: ☐ Cheque
> Credit Card ☐ Visa ☐ Mastercard ☐ AMEX ☐ Discover ☐ Novus

Card number:_____

Name on card: _____Exp date: _____/___